UNDERSTANDING
The Real
TEACHINGS of
MOSES and JESUS

INTERPRETATIONS BY DARA NDU

EMEKA UDE, J.

ASPIRE
PUBLISHING HUB LLC.

Library of Congress Control Number: 2024912619

ISBN
978-1-964393-51-3 (Paperback)
978-1-964393-52-0 (eBook)

Table of Contents

PREFACE

One of the greatest challenges Jesus faced in the course of His Ministry on Earth, was the unfortunate misinterpretations of the Laws of Moses by Jewish religious leaders. He had at one point assured them in Matt 5:18-19 (NKJV) *"Do not think I came to destroy the Law or the Prophets. I did not come to destroy but to fulfill. For assuredly, I say to you, till heaven and earth pass away, one jot or one tittle will by no means pass from the Law till all is fulfilled"*. But in Matt 15:3, He accused them: *"Why do you also transgress the commandment of God because of your tradition?"*

The Synoptic Gospels contain a litany of altercations between Jesus and the Jews concerning incorrect interpretations of the Laws of Moses. The Jewish religious leaders had replaced the "doctrines" of God with the "commandments of men". And through the years, these false interpretations of men had gradually taken the rightful place of the true Laws of God. In fact these incorrect interpretations eventually carried a high price: they cost John the Baptist his head; and they got Jesus nailed to the cross.

Unfortunately today, we find that Christians are also repeating the same mistakes of the past. Christian scholars all over the World have differed in understanding of very critical Scriptural teachings– everyone dissecting the "Word" as he feels. The Scripture has suffered carnal, physical and literal interpretations in the hands of these "religious merchants", resulting in confusion, delusion, needless controversy and ignorance in the body of Christ.

In our first book (an autobiography) titled, *Dara Ndu: The Long-Awaited Christ*, we introduced DARA NDU, who had announced to the World that He is the prophesied and long-awaited Christ; that He took human form in the great Igboland of Nigeria. According to Him, "*I spoke in the body of Melchezedek; I spoke in the body of Moses; I spoke in the body of Jesus. And now, I took up the name, DARA NDU*".

Dara Ndu enthused, "*when mankind abandons the spiritual rendition of the Bible and begins to take every verse carnally, the Messiah appears. It is only the Messiah that has the secret key to unlocking the spiritual meaning of the Biblical verses. No human being can correctly interpret the Holy Bible except He that owns it – the Messiah. The Words of the Scripture is Me; the Words are talking about me*".

In *Understanding the Real Teachings of Moses and Jesus*, Dara Ndu aims at correctly interpreting what He spoke in the Books of the Law; the Synoptic Gospels and the Revelations to Apostle John (the Beloved).

Understanding the Real Teachings of Moses and Jesus was crafted in very simple sentences, but with great unction and power. It is rendered predominantly in simple English Language, but with a tinge of Igbo language – indigenous dialect spoken by Dara Ndu. Of course, caution was applied not to inundate the readers with needless books, chapters and verses of the Bible.

Consequently, the exposition was limited to the following books containing messages spoken by Dara Ndu Himself–

Genesis	
Exodus	Matthew
Numbers	Luke
Deuteronomy	John
Joshua	Revelation

Understanding the Real Teachings of Moses and Jesus is a reference book; and therefore it is recommended to be read alongside the Bible. Scripture quotations are taken from The Living Bible, except otherwise stated.

It is my sincere prayer that by using this reference material, you will be filled with the knowledge of God's Will in all wisdom and spiritual understanding; that you may walk worthy of the Lord, fully pleasing Him; being fruitful in every good work, and increasing in the knowledge of God. And as you combine "the knowledge of His Will", with "spiritual understanding", then you will be "translated" out of the "darkness" of ignorance and misinterpretations of the Word of God into the light of the true "Faith". Col.1:9-13 (NKJV) (**paraphrases mine**).

Emeka Ude, J

THE TEACHINGS
OF MOSES

GENESIS

CHAPTER 1 – PHYSICAL CREATION

Verse 1 The story started with the conclusion or summary– *"In the beginning, God created the heaven and earth."* (KJV) *"When God began creating the heavens and the earth...."* (The Living Bible).

'Heavens' refer to the many abodes of the Spirit– since It resides in the hearts of all living things. And all the living things can only be found exclusively on earth.

Verse 2 Before the processes of creation commenced, two things were already in existence – Water and Fire (the Spirit of God or the Power of God). The Ocean or Deep or Water was not like the water we are used to. On the contrary, it was dark, chaotic, without arrangement. Fire, or its characteristics, was interwoven with it. Both had no beginning or an end – but were inseparable.

Creation of all the living things and the earth occurred from a drama that took place between water (*Mmiri*) and Fire (*Oku*). The union or sex between them gave rise to The Spirit – *MMUO*. This is the foundation of Creation– which the whole universe today worship as '*GOD*'.

Mmuo: *Mm*, was severed from *Mmiri* (water); *uo*, severed from *Oku* (Fire).

On its own, the water has the duty of making Laws and Constitutions for the Creation processes. But these Constitutions are in darkness and cannot be useful until the Fire gives Consent, Direction or Authority. It is the Fire that has the force, or aggression or positivity to give Light to the Constitution and shatter the darkness, and hence give vent to the commencement of Creation.

Verse 3-5 This consent or authority came with its First Word – *OOOOOM*!!! With this word, Lightning occurred and darkness gave way. At its command for the Light to be used, Thunder arose bringing about arrangement and placement of the earth and creatures therein.

Verse 6-31 Commentaries:

a. It took The Spirit (*Mmuo*), 8,400,000 years to complete the First Creation. Six (6) different species of Living Things were created inside the space called the Earth– (in this order):

- Aquatics
- Plants/ Trees
- Insects
- Birds
- Animals
- Human Beings

b. The Earth is surrounded or submerged in the Water (Ocean), but separated by nine (9) decking up the sky and nine (9) decking below (*Verse 6-10*). See 2 Peter 3:5-6. The following words in Igbo Language originated from this creative activity:

'Uwa'– O walu ya awa, (The Spirit separated the Waters, and the Earth emerged)

'Ala'– O si ka O nodu Mmiri ala, ala a puta (The Spirit decided to sit on the Waters, Land emerged)

'Igwe'– O gwedo Mmiri n'elu, a kpoba ya Igwe (The Spirit expanded the Waters above, and it is called the Sky)

c. Therefore, we are living inside The Spirit. That is why Apostle Paul wondered the kind of building to give 'GOD' when we are living inside It.

d. When the minds (thoughts) of people living in a particular area melts, the snow that forms the first decking melts and *rain falls*.

e. The Stars in the sky do not exist physically. They represent the eyes of the creatures in the Earth. It is just like using mirror to build ceiling in a house. Whatever you place on the floor of the house is reflected on the ceiling.

f. Water and Fire agreed to fill the Earth in order to prevent it from being desolate. The first living specie to be created was Aquatics. The Spirit lived 900,000 years in the bodies of these creatures before it entered into or created or became the next – i.e. Plants and Trees, etc.

	Bodies Created	Species of created bodies	Years the Spirit lived in the bodies	Stars that represent the bodies
1	Aquatics	900,000	900,000	900,000
2	Plants and Trees	2,000,000	2,000,000	2,000,000
3	Insects	1,100,000	1,100,000	1,100,000
4	Birds	1,000,000	1,000,000	1,000,000
5	Animals	3,000,000	3,000,000	3,000,000
6	Human Beings	400,000	400,000	400,000
Total		8,400,000	8,400,000	8,400,000

Please note that 400,000 species of the created human beings represent 400,000 levels of consciousness in Body and Mind.

This Creation Process is called *Involution* and *Evolution*. Involution is the movement of The Spirit from one body to another. Hitherto, Evolution had been described as a process whereby the body of a Living thing changes from one to the next. This assertion by Charles Darwin is a farce. It is a falsehood. It is anti-creation for the body of specie to transform into another body without the process of death. The body of specie must die before The Spirit creates or enters the next body. For example, when Chimpanzee or Ape reached its extinction, i.e., matured to its final level of existence, it died before The Spirit created Man.

g. Man is the zenith or the greatest of all creatures. There is no being like Man. Even the so-called Angels bow for Man. In Igbo language, Man is referred to as *Mma Ndu* – the Beauty of Life, *not Madu as it is pronounced today,* Verse 28.

Verse 29-31 The Spirit provides for the adaptation and sustenance of the Living things created.

CHAPTER 2 – THE LAWS OF CREATION

Chapter Two should have come before Chapter One. Whereas Chapter One is the Foundation of Creation, Chapter Two is The Laws of Creation. Naturally the Laws should set the tone for the Foundation.

Verse 1-3 The *Six (6) days of Creation* as recorded in Chapter One refers to the Six (6) bodies that were created. See the '*Wedding in Cana*' in the Book of John Chapter Two. When the last body (Man) realizes he is spirit, his mind becomes one with The Spirit. Then the mind is at rest. It ceases work (struggles) and goes into its rest or Jubilee. This is attained in the Seventh body (*Seventh day*), i.e., self-realization or consciousness. The mind or the person is said to have "*known itself*" or attained *Salvation*, Verse 3.

Verse 7 *"Dust"* refers to the five (5) Elements of Creation namely (in this order): Water, Fire, Earth, Ether (Space) and Sky.

"Living Soul/ Person" is the Mind.

What was created is the Mind or Body. The Spirit was not created. See Chapter 1:2 – The Spirit (Water and Fire) are the only *Two Uncreated Beings*. The Spirit gives Mind and Body power and Life. Water and Fire have everything they needed to exist as living creatures – they are self-sustaining. They are *Life, Knowledge and Bliss*, but do not experience them. They therefore decided to create physical universe in order to enjoy their natures inside themselves.

So what The Spirit did was to shoot out those parts of the body from itself. The Spirit as a matter of fact created itself in those species – from aquatics to human bodies (Self-Reproduction). It is not as if a human body, for example, was literally molded and air breathed into it.

Verse 8 The Spirit formed the Heart (*Garden*) in the Body (*Eden*), in the Right hand side (*East*) and placed in the Heart (*Garden*), the Mind (*Man*) he had formed. Therefore, the first thing The Spirit created was the Mind; and the first thing the Mind has is The Spirit.

Verse 9 The Spirit created other parts of the body namely:

a. The Tree of Knowledge of Good and Evil (The Tree of Conscience) is the Mind; referred to as *Ikpe Uche*, in Igbo language.

    The Tree of Life is The Spirit.

b. Intellect is *Mkpoko Uche* or *Echiche*.

c. Senses are *Ogugu Echiche/Uche*.

Mkpoko Uche or Intellect collates and sieves what the Mind has created. *Ogugu Echiche/Uche i.e.,* Senses, regulate or measure what the Mind does.

d. Memory is *Cheta*

e. Body is *ahu*

The Tree of knowledge of good and evil, intellect, senses, memory and body are the beautiful trees (pleasant to the sight) that surround the garden (heart).

The Mind is in the head (Brain is Mind); and The Spirit is in the Heart (*O mmuo a? – Is it this Spirit?* – pointing at your heart). Remember, the heart is the abode of The Spirit.

Different classes of people use different terms to describe the same thing: Mind

Class of people	Term used
Scientists	Brain
Spiritual	Soul
Metaphysicists	Mind

Verse 10-14 Blood and water flow into all parts of the body including hands, legs, etc. The four (4)

rivers – Pishon, Gihon, Hidekel and Euphrates – are describing the physical human being.

Verse 15 After creating human body, it was entrusted into the hands of the Mind to look after. John 2:7-10.

Verse 16-17 A person can use his senses, intellect, memory and body as freely as he likes, but the moments he '*eats*' the fruits of the Mind (i.e., when the Mind or person realizes it must be one with The Spirit) all the passions, carnality and materialism of life will die (see Genesis 3:5).

Recall *Verse 9.* The Mind is the tree of conscience or of good and evil. It is the Mind that needs to be salvaged. But why did The Spirit command that it must not be tasted? This is a case of negative positivism – one needs to think and work hard for his salvation.

The Mind is the creating power of The Spirit. If it follows The Spirit, a person attains salvation. But if it follows the body he becomes Satan or Devil.

Verse 18-25 Commentaries

First Creation: It took 8,400,000 years for The Spirit to complete the First Creation. The Spirit lived the stipulated number of years in the body of each specie before entering the next. In the case of human being, the first human species (female) was engaged in self-reproduction i.e., it migrated into self until it clocked 200,000 years or levels of consciousness. Thereafter, it migrated into the male body. The male body in turn completed another 200,000 years to bring the levels of human consciousness to 400,000 years. This completed the First Creation for human beings.

It was after this first 400,000 years that man and woman began sexual reproduction. This is called Subsequent Creation/Development – Procreation. Of course the male body could not relate with the female body without completing its 200,000 years.

Verse 18 This verse is talking about the companionship of Fire (Man) and Water (Woman). Fire is the symbol of man and Water, symbol of woman.

Verse 19-20 The Mind was given the responsibility of giving names to created things according to the characteristics of those things.

Verse 21-24 Man came out of woman. See the commentary on the first creation. Woman – female body was first created. After 200,000 years, it migrated into the male body. Recall also that Fire and Water were interwoven before the physical creation – ("The Spirit of God – Fire – was brooding over the Water" Gen.1:2). Fire came out of Water to give Light to its Laws and Constitutions. It was their agreement, in view of the expansive nature of Water that it comes out first as female body.

Nevertheless both are equal. None is greater than the other. Their functions, duties and responsibilities are different but complimentary and interdependent.

Verse 25 Man and woman were both naked and not ashamed – a demonstration of oneness and togetherness of Fire and Water, bearing one name – The Spirit.

CHAPTER 3 – SALVATION, SELF-REALIZATION, SELF-CONSCIOUSNESS

Chapter Three discusses the relationship between The Spirit, Mind and Body vis-a-vis Salvation, Self-realization and Self-Consciousness of an individual. In Igbo parlance, The Spirit is referred to as *Mmuo*; the Mind is *Mmuo-Okike*, whereas the Body is called *Mmuo-Ozi*.

The message here is that a person must realize himself as the Spirit in order to attain salvation. The Mind and Body must agree to follow The Spirit for an individual to realize himself.

Verse 1-3 Definition of figures and Characters used:

- Serpent or Snake is the Mind
- Eve is the Physical Body
- Adam is The Spirit; *Adamus*, in Latin means Spirit

In *Verse 1*, the Mind was asking the body whether The Spirit doesn't want it – the body – to know or realize itself. It is the Mind that tells the body what to do.

Verse 2 The body replied, "We can use our senses, memory, intellect, conscience, body – (these are the products of the Mind)– as we like. But the day we realize ourselves as the Spirit, the physical passions and carnality of the body dies."

The Spirit intended the Mind to search for It. It did not want to make Salvation easy for the Mind. That is why It warned them not to "eat" it. It is a kind of test. Recall that the Tree of Life should give Life and not death. So why would The Spirit suggest they would die?

Verse 4-5 The Mind told the body that it will not die. Of course, the Mind is right for it had been with the Spirit for a long time. The Mind knows that as soon as the body realizes itself, it (the body) will become spiritual i.e., be like The Spirit. And all the pressures, stresses, struggles and rat race in the world of matter will cease. The body will be at rest.

Verse 6 The body has realized that as he ate the fruit, all praises were accorded to him. All the ceremonies take place in the body even though it is the Mind that does all the work.

Verse 7 The husband of the woman (body) is the Mind. The Spirit is the husband of both Mind and Body. The body via the eyes, ears, other senses, memory etc, received the spiritual knowledge of self-realization. The body and mind had agreed and had followed ("eaten") the Spirit. The Three must agree to be One.

You become naked when you realize yourself as The Spirit. It happened to Solomon. When he realized himself, he lamented, "Vanity upon vanity, all is vanity" (*Eccle 1:2 KJV*). When Paul came to that consciousness, all stubbornness and doubts ceased – *Acts of the Apostles*.

The nakedness refers to awareness of their emptiness despite all the material possessions and properties. When man discovers he must abandon all these mundane possessions, he was unhappy and ashamed of himself.

To own properties is not condemnable, but these physical pursuits must be carried out in accordance with the knowledge of the Spirit – the correct teachings of the Messiah. Money is not evil. It is good as a means of exchange, but must not be acquired exclusively and with total disregard to the Laws of Creation.

Verse 8 After the realization of oneself, test for the man begins. "*Hiding*" refers to avoiding those things you were doing when you hadn't realized yourself as Spirit.

Verse 9-10 You become tired of those things. You are no more impressed or carried away by those things that are mundane. When you know the Truth, you stay away from material acquisition and life of carnality.

Verse 11 The Spirit continues to test man. Recall the Temptation of Jesus. When Jesus realized Himself as (The Incarnate of) The Spirit, there was great battle/conflict between His Body and Mind.

Verse 12 Adam here refers to the Mind, admitting that it was the body that possesses the instruments (eyes, ears, memory etc) that receive the spiritual knowledge of self-realization.

Verse 14-16 The Laws of the Mind and Body – As soon you know The Spirit, there will be physical suffering; otherwise you will go back to the 'world'. It is only those things that The Spirit wants the body to enjoy that will come to the person.

Verse 15 There will be a conflict between the Mind and body. The desires of both will never be the same again. The body will experience pains in whatever it does. Notwithstanding the desires of the body, the Mind shall control it.

Verse 17 Adam here refers to the Mind. The Mind works hard to create all physical things.

Verse 19 The body and mind will go to the grave at separation from the Spirit (i.e., physical death).

Verse 20-21 Further Commentaries on Creation.

Verse 22-24 Repetition of the stories earlier told on Creation.

CHAPTER 4 – CARNALITY: CONSEQUENCES OF BODY FOLLOWING THE MIND

- *The Story of Cain and Abel*

The story relates the consequences of body accepting to follow the dictates of the Mind. If the body does the bidding of the Mind or both uniting, an odd (curse) shall be placed in the way of the Mind. It cannot make progress towards spirituality. It could be earthbound (vagabond) and possibly become evil.

Verse 1 The Spirit – God – is the goddess of sex. The consolidation of Water and Fire (Negative and Positive) brought about Creation.

Verse 2 The Spirit gave rise to Mind and Body.

- Cain is Mind;
- Abel is Body.
- Adam is The Spirit, symbolizing Fire.
- Eve symbolizes Water.

Verse 4 Abel tithed the best part of its heart to the Spirit. The Mind is always jealous of the body because the body takes the glory meant for the Mind. It is the body that shows the manifestations of the work of the Mind and really enjoys its creations.

Verse 5 The Mind struggles within itself regarding what to give to The Spirit. It thinks out what to do. But after it had decided, the body carries it out or administers it in its entirety. It – the Body – does not have a choice of its own. It always administers what the Mind eventually decides to do. In other words, the Mind creates (*Mmuo-Okike*), but the body administers (*Mmuo-Ozi).*

Verse 6, 7 The Spirit advises the Mind.

Verse 8 The Mind 'kills' the body. Please note that this is not physical killing/murder. It is the body's acceptance of the dictates of the Mind. In the same vein, when the Spirit "kills" the Mind, the Mind accepts the dictates of the Spirit.

Verse 9 The Spirit queried the Mind concerning the body's acceptance of its dictates. It is indeed terrible for the Mind to conquer the body.

Verse 10-12 With the coming together of the Mind and the body, the former could no longer function properly. Man has thus become carnal and mundane.

Verse 13-14 *"Farm"* here refers to the body. When the Spirit takes over the mind and the body, i.e. when awareness dawns on the mind, it can no longer use the body the way it likes. Limitations (curses, punishment) have now being imposed on the mind. He is therefore stopped or precluded from enjoying those things (physical and material) he had hitherto relished in. The mind discovered this and then lamented before the Lord.

Verse 15 But the Spirit assured him that whosoever mocks at him as a result of his awareness or self-realization will be met with more terrible curses and punishment.

Verse 16 The mind – Cain – became a wanderer (wilderness life). The mind is actually at the right hand side of the body *".....east of Eden".*

Verse 17 Cain's wife here refers to the body.

Verse 18-26 The stories of Enoch and his genealogy (descendants) are subsequent bodies in later ages.

CHAPTER 5 – CONTINUATION OF THE STORY ON CREATION

This Chapter repeats the story on the First Creation. For greater details, go back to Chapter One and Two.

The figures mentioned here are the periods The Spirit lived in various created bodies. But the compilers stated them wrongly.

For avoidance of doubts, it took The Spirit 8,400,000 years to complete the First Creation.

CHAPTER 6 – THE STORY OF END -TIME AND CREATION IN THE TIME OF NOAH, THE MESSIAH

This Chapter is a two-pronged story – End Time (Verses 1-13) and Physical Creation (Verse 14-22) recorded by Moses concerning the time of Noah, the Messiah.

Verses 1-13 End Time: A human era is a period of 2,000 years, divided into four (4) phase periods of 500 years each.

Phase	Age	Percentage of Righteousness	Percentage of Evil
First	Golden	Above 75	Below 25
Second	Silver	50	50
Third	Bronze	25	75
Fourth & Last	Iron/Khali	Below 5	Above 95

Messiahs always appear during the end of the last 500 years, i.e Iron or Khali Age; usually described as the End Time, End of a Human Era or the Last days of 2,000 years. This period is always characterized by a concomitant preponderance of evil, dominated by wickedness and high sex perversion.

Evil was at its zenith when Noah, the Messiah appeared. His three sons represent the Trinity – *Mmuo, Mmuo-Okike* and *Mmuo-Ozi*. Noah's Ark or Boat can be referred to as the Body. Noah was to physically build up the Mind of Mankind through the teachings of the Laws of the Spirit.

The boat can also be referred to as houses where the saved ones will stay during the imminent and inevitable destruction that will bring about the end of the Age.

Verse 14-22 **First Creation** – Before the physical creation, the Universe was covered by flood, i.e. water. Compliers used the word "destruction". The ark/boat refers to the earth. The two (pair) of each kind of species represent Fire and Water – the two (2) uncreated beings that formed the Foundation of Creation.

Verse 15, 16 On earth, there are three (3) different levels of Consciousness –

- The Spirit, which is the Upper deck
- The Mind, which is the middle deck, and
- The Body, which is the Bottom deck

All living species have body, mind and spirit. The mind in other specie – aquatics to animals – is referred to as instinct or *echiche nta* or *chi nta*.

Verse 17 Read this verse alongside verse 2 of Chapter One, "*…the earth was at first a shapeless, chaotic mass…*dark *ocean*" – TLB. Shapeless, chaotic and darkness are synonymous to destruction because no object, specie or creature was in existence. The earth was covered with ocean and everything (earth's content) was literally destroyed – chaotic and dark.

CHAPTER 7– CONTINUATION OF THE STORY OF CREATION

The story of Creation continues. The *'40 days and nights'* are the 400,000 levels of Consciousness a human body lives on earth. It is not feasible for rain to fall consistently for 40 days. Noah did not live for *600* years. No human body can exist up till that age. Besides, that was during an Iron Age, where human Life Span is very short: Noah had become a matured human being before the end time.

LIFE SPAN:

Golden Age	Silver Age	Bronze Age	Iron Age
150-200 Years	100-150 Years	90-120 Years	55-120 Years

The highest Life Span in Iron Age is 70 years. Premature death occurs below 50 years of age. Climate, diet and life style determine a man's life span. In fact vegetarians live longer than non-vegetarians.

Rain in spiritual context means war, battles or trouble. The Spirit uses allegories, figures or objects to give messages especially when the audience cannot bear direct instructions.

Therefore when you dream of being beaten by rainfall, it means somebody will insult you or you will quarrel with him. An English idiomatic expression says, *"Raining insult on somebody"*

When you dive into a river and touches the bed of the river, it means you will discover something in real life. But when you are swimming or afloat a river, you are in trouble.

Verse 18 Boat/Ark/Ship refers to the earth. After creation, earth was surrounded by ocean (water)– Gen 1:1-10.

Commentaries – There is a lot of mix-up in this Chapter. A lot of objects and figures were used to render the story on creation; and end time. Only the Messiah can break these codes. A similar scenario occurred in Chapter 24 of the Gospel according to Matthew. Jesus told the stories of End Time and Coming of the Messiah together.

CHAPTER 8– CREATION AND MANKIND

The story of creation is still being told here.

Verse 15-19 Refer to Chapter 1:28

Verse 20 *Altar* represents the Heart; *animals and birds* represent the senses, memory, intellect and body – that are sacrifices to the Spirit. When a person realizes himself, it pleases the Spirit (The Lord).

CHAPTER 9– LAWS OF CREATION: DO'S AND DON'TS

The Laws of Creation are repeated in this Chapter. These Laws are taught by Noah – the incarnate of the Supreme Spirit. So when you read that God told Noah or God blessed Noah, etc, always bear in mind that these are the activities of Noah, since he stands in the place of the Supreme Spirit.

Verse 12-17 The last sign before destruction of earth is Rainbow and seven days warning. See also Chapter 7:10

Verse 20-27 This was a revelation of Noah wherein he teaches that the mind that follows the body is always cursed.

CHAPTER 10

This chapter chronicles the descendants of the sons of Noah.

CHAPTER 11– CREATION AND ABUSE OF LANGUAGE (S)

Language is a seed of the Spirit. The Spirit owns all languages. No language is man-made. If a man is not alive, he cannot speak a language. For instance, when you answer a call with a response like, O *Mmuo a?* (Is it this Spirit?), you would point at the heart – the abode of the Spirit. It is thus the Spirit that is speaking – recognizing itself when it is called.

Indeed, the speech manifests through the organs of the body – the mind and body being the vehicles of the Spirit. The Spirit empowers both. If the Spirit moves away from the body, the latter cannot speak anymore.

Creation emanated because the Spirit (Water and Fire) desired to enjoy or express itself outside itself. Hence after Creation of Man, mankind had the potentialities of speaking (a language (s)). Even though one person may not be able to understand the other, but the Spirit must express himself in that body created.

Language (s) is a seed in The Spirit – which manifests itself at creation. For example, a bean seed on its own does not have leaves, root, stem flowers etc. But when the seed is planted, all those parts sprout out. Language is therefore, in the Spirit, but begins to manifest when the Spirit takes on a body form, i.e., when the body is created.

- ### *Abuse of Language at End-Time*

Verse 1-9 At the end of each age, there is always the tendency of mankind speaking one language. This leads to their efforts towards working against God. But after the Final Judgment, they will begin to speak different languages.

- ### *Igbo Language and Creation*

Every time a Messiah comes, he uses the oldest and the most superior language to explain Creation and bring about Salvation. For instance, Jesus spoke Aramaic. Aramaic language is no longer spoken in any part of the earth. It is lost, but has been replaced by 'Hebrew'.

Igbo Language is already at the verge of loss and extinction. Igbo race no longer wants to speak it. Of all known languages today, Igbo language is the oldest. Others have either gone into extinction or are being modified. But Igbo language still retains its original form. That is why it is the most superior.

Let us consider the word, "*Oladikpo*". Igbo language will retain the compound letter, *kp*. Yoruba language will remove *k* but pronounce the word as *Oladikpo*. Nevertheless they will write the word as *Oladipo*. With the word '*Labour*', the Americans will remove '*u*'. These races (Yoruba, Americans, etc) want to write the words to align with their style of speaking.

Besides, other languages were derived from Igbo. It has neither beginning nor end. It is as old as the Spirit. It is the language of Creation and therefore, the language of the Spirit. This explains why the Messiah, in the new name and new body of DARA NDU uses Igbo language to teach the sciences of Creation and bring about the message of Salvation. During Jesus' time Aramaic (Hebrew today) was the superior language because Jesus used it to teach Creation and Salvation. That also explains the reason Christendom today still trace deep biblical understanding/meanings to Hebrew language.

• **Commentaries**

a.   If '*ni*' (Hausa), '*me*' (English), '*emi*' (Yoruba), '*Mmuo a*' (Igbo) etc., originally spoken in any race does not stand for the Spirit, that language is fake.

b.   *Sanskrit* – Sans means God; Krit stands for…'come to human consumption.' Therefore, Sanskrit means anything that man can put into use or consumption. Example, languages, plank made from trees, chairs etc. There is no particular language known as Sanskrit.

CHAPTER 12 – MANKIND AND ITS ACTIVITIES

The Spirit permits the Mind to follow the body in the enjoyment of the physical attractions of life. However, when the Mind realizes itself i.e., when the Spirit takes the Mind back, there is bound to be difficulties (punishment, plaques) inflicted on it.

Put differently, whcn a person realizes himself as Spirit, i.e. becomes spiritual, he suffers physical deprivation, economic stress and lack. All the attractions of this physical life disappear.

Verse 1-10 Abram here represents The Spirit; Egypt symbolizes the body; Pharaoh, the King of Egypt stands for the Mind.

Sarai, Abram's wife is the Mind that follows the Spirit. The people of Egypt are the senses, memory, intellect, etc.

That Abram went to Egypt means that the Spirit is inside the body.

The Bible is primarily talking about three levels of a man's activities in Creation:

- The Spiritual Man
- The Mental/Mind man i.e 'Spiritually' minded man
- The Physical/Body man i.e 'Carnally' minded man

Please do not remove your mind or thought away from these scenarios whenever you are reading the Bible.

Verse 11-16 The Spirit urged the spiritually minded not to tell the carnally minded that He was her husband. On the contrary, she should tell him that she is the Intellect (his sister).

Simply put, The Spirit, just like the Mind uses Intellect. In some religions, God is described as The Supreme Intelligence. In the Book of Exodus Chapter Two, it was recorded that Pharaoh's daughter discovered Moses. Pharaoh's daughter here represents Intellect, meaning that Moses uses superior Intelligence to work.

Verse 17 At realization of Itself as the Spirit, the Mind experiences difficulties – deprivation, lack, economic stress etc. Physical attractions of Life fade away. A person no longer needs them since he is going 'home'.

Verse 18 When the Mind discovered he must follow the Spirit, he regretted wasting time for a long period acquiring physical but perishable items/articles.

Verse 19-20 *"And Pharaoh sent them out"*– The mind finally succumbs to the dictates of the Spirit.

CHAPTER 13– EMERGENCE OF LOT AS THE MESSIAH

LOT emerged as the Incarnate of Abram (the Spirit). Lot stands for the Spirit inhabited in a human body. A human became Spirit i.e. Messiah.

Verse 11 When the Spirit (Abram) and the Messiah (Lot) separated, there was no longer *duality*. The Spirit became Messiah; but both are One. Jesus once said, "I and my Father are One."

Verse 14 The Spirit created and therefore owns every creature on earth.

CHAPTER 14– BRIEF INTRODUCTION OF MELCHIZEDEK AS MESSIAH

Verse 14-17 The Spirit is the guide and guard of the mission of Lot.

Verse 18-20 The Spirit handed power to Melchizedek as Messiah. Not much was mentioned here about him, until in *Chapter Seven of the New Testament Book of Hebrew.*

CHAPTER 15– STORY ON CREATION

This is a drama (conversation) between the Spirit and Mind concerning physical creation.

Verse 2-3 'Steward (a member) of…house' refer to Mind and Body. How can the mind and body inherit his wisdom? The Spirit wants to create what is like it (Like begets Like). This was fulfilled when Sarah begot Isaac. Sarah and Isaac are spiritual minds; when compared to Hagar and Ishmael, representing physical senses. *Agwo ga-amu agwo (Like begets like).*

Verse5 '*Seed*' (descendants) refer to spiritual minds.

Verse 13 400 years refer to 400,000 years that the Spirit will live in human bodies before the latter attains consciousness, awareness or self-realization.

In summary, when the Spiritual minds realized themselves, physical attractions of life will be taken away (i.e. become oppressed).

CHAPTER 16– REPETITION OF THE STORY OF PHYSICAL CREATION

The story of Creation is repeated here in another form.

Verse 1, 2 Sarah – the spiritual Mind urged Abram – The Spirit – (both are Spirit) for Children (Creation to take effect). Abram (Fire) agreed with Sarah (Water).

Verse 3-15 The Supreme Spirit (consent of Fire and Water; male and female or positive and negative) took the form of Hagar – the Creative Mind (God); who now issued out the Creation – Ishmael.

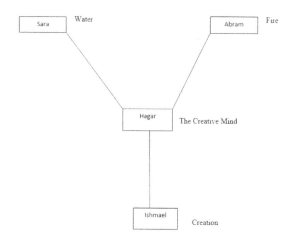

Please see Chapter One: on Physical Creation; and Jesus' Miracle at Wedding in Cana – John 2

CHAPTER 17– THE SPIRIT'S COVENANT OF CIRCUMCISION WITH MANKIND

Circumcision referred to here is not a physical mutilation or cutting of male genital foreskin. It is the circumcision of heart in order to earn Salvation. The whole duty of Man on earth is to realize himself as Spirit.

CHAPTERS 18 AND 19– LOT AND CLOSE OF AGE

At the end of every 2,000 years, the reigning Messiah brings the Age to an end through an Imminent but inevitable fire disaster.

Chapter 18 Lot warned his people through his teachings and admonitions, but they turned deaf ears and continued to live in evil

Chapter 19:1-29 Disaster struck. Sodom and Gomorrah was utterly destroyed.

Verse 26 Lot's wife could not follow through. She went back to evil and was destroyed alongside.

Verse 30-38 Story of Creation: Again Lot repeated the story on Creation here. Lot represents the Spirit; his firstborn daughter stands for the Mind; and the younger daughter, the body. Mind is always the first to accept what is to be created. It is the creative power of the Spirit – giving rise to the body.

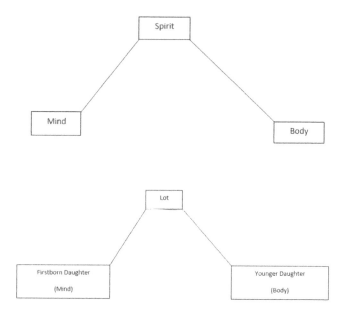

Pictorially, the Spirit gave rise to Mind and Body; just as Lot had two daughters.

- ***Commentaries:***

Chapter 18 Lot, the Messiah is the incarnate of Abram, the Supreme Spirit. They are One. There is no more duality having separated from each other as seen in Chapter 13.

These Chapters are records of the messages (Visions, revelations) received by Lot, the Messiah. There was no physical conversation between Abram and the Angels on one hand (Chapter 18) or between Lot and Angels on the other (Chapter 19).

CHAPTER 20– MANKIND AND ITS ACTIVITIES

Reference: See Chapter 12

When the Mind becomes tired, he surrenders to the Spirit together with all he has – senses, memory, intellect, body etc. Otherwise he will never know peace.

King Abimelech refers to Mind, King of the Body (Gerar).

CHAPTER 21– STORY OF CREATION AGAIN

The drama of Creation played by the Spirit, Mind and Body continues. The entire Bible is talking about Creation of Man as Trinity and the relationship subsisting among this tripartite being.

Verse 1-9 Abraham, the Spirit begets Isaac, the Mind. Recall that Sarah is the spiritual mind which now begets Isaac, another spiritual mind – the mind that follows the Spirit. Like, attracts like.

Verse 10-21 "Cast out this bondwoman and her son…" Recall that Hagar and her son, Ishmael are physical minds. They are the minds that follow the physical body. When it is said that Lucifer was driven down the earth, it refers to the Mind that has taken to the dictates of the physical body.

Verse 27 "Gifts" are senses, memory, intellect, etc. The Spirit gave to the Mind (Abimelech)…the other beautiful trees around the garden, Chapter 2:9.

CHAPTER 22– CONQUER YOUR MIND

When a man sacrifices his mind to the Spirit, i.e. when a man conquers his mind by realizing himself as Spirit, his body will not have a choice than to obey.

The body administers what the mind creates through senses, intellect and memory etc. If these are conquered, the body becomes the sacrificial lamb/ram.

Verse 1-14 Wood refers to senses, intellect, memory and conscience. These are the avenues through which the mind operates. Altar is the heart – the abode of the Spirit. This is where the Mind is offered as a sacrifice. Ram is the physical body.

Verse 15-18 When you have sacrificed your mind to the Spirit, you have indeed tithed. Tithing is giving at least one-tenth of your heart to the Spirit. If you sacrifice your mind to the Spirit, you earn Salvation. See the Book of Malachi 3:10-12.

CHAPTER 23 – (NO SPIRITUAL VALUE TO MAN)

CHAPTER 24 – STORY OF CREATION CONTINUES....

Like, begets like. Spiritual Mind– Isaac– creates similar spiritual mind, Rebekah. He married from his father's (Abraham) relative. The Canaanite (local) girls are physical minds.

CHAPTER 25 – RELATIONSHIP BETWEEN MIND AND BODY

The Mind serves the body. It also drives the body. It is the mind that labors while the body enjoys. The body administers all that the mind creates. The Mind is always at the desert/wilderness – i.e. always pondering, thinking and building castles in the air. But the body administers or makes use of what is available.

The body is always at the receiving end. It enjoys all the blessings. It takes all the praises. It enjoys all that the mind creates. If the body gets diseased, the Mind rests.

Esau represents the Mind, while Jacob is the body. Rebekah played the role of the Intellect, as will be seen in Chapter 27.

CHAPTER 26 – MANKIND AND ITS ACTIVITIES

Reference: Chapter 12 and 20

CHAPTER 27 – RELATIONSHIP BETWEEN MIND AND BODY

Reference: Chapter 25

CHAPTERS 28 AND 29 – STORY OF CREATION

Like, attracts like. Jacob here is spiritual mind – of the same lineage with Isaac. Similar story of Creation is repeated here but with different nomenclatures describing the Trinity. Reference: Chapter 24.

CHAPTERS 30-36— REPETITION OF THE STORY OF CREATION

Reference: Chapter 16

Chapter 30:1– The Mind is barren.

CHAPTER 37— GAINS OF MIND THAT FOLLOWS THE SPIRIT

Joseph is a spiritual mind or person. Mind can also be expressed as a person – since Spirit, mind and body are talking about a person.

Verse 1-11 A spiritual person sees visions, receives revelations and hears from the Spirit. Joseph's brothers are physical mind – they are carnally minded and are jealous because of Joseph's abilities.

Verse 12-33 The mind – spiritual and physical – has conflict within itself. Sometimes, your mind urges you to do an evil thing, but at another time, changes and advises against it. Its final choice (between good or evil) determines whether it is spiritual or physical.

Verse 6, 7, 9 Commentaries: Meaning of Joseph's dreams – The physical minds must submit (bow) to the Spirit.

CHAPTER 38— (NO SPIRITUAL VALUE TO MAN)

CHAPTER 39— GAINS OF MIND THAT FOLLOWS THE SPIRIT

Verse 1-6 *"Joseph arrived Egypt"*– the Spiritual Mind in the physical body. We are talking about a person in this

World. Because he is spiritual, he is still perfect despite being in the body (prison). Every spiritual mind in the physical body is in prison.

Jesus said to his disciples, "*You are in the World but not of the World.*" We are in the world but must not be carried away by carnality and gross materialism.

Potiphar represents a physical body that learns from the spiritual mind (Joseph). Even though a physical body, it has come to know the Spirit.

Verse 7-21 Potiphar's wife is also a physical body which lures the spiritual mind (Joseph) to abandon the Spirit for sensuality. Joseph resisted, "*My Master entrusted me with everything in the entire household.*" Once you resist the lure and temptation of the physical body, there will be conflict, stress and difficulties.

CHAPTER 40– SPIRITUAL MIND ASSISTS THE BODY

Spiritual Mind sees visions and interprets dreams. Like the spiritual mind, the physical mind can see vision and revelation but they may not be able to interpret them. The body makes use of the visions for protection and economic advantage. It is always interested in knowing its tomorrow. The mind receives the vision from the Spirit but the body tells it.

Emeka Ude, J.

CHAPTER 41– SPIRITUAL PERSONS INHERIT THE EARTH

The spiritual mind became the King of the body. Pharaoh, the physical mind is no longer in charge. Both minds are always contesting for the rulership of the physical body.

Verse 28-36 But the spiritual mind subdued the physical mind by proffering solution to life problem (a feat which the physical mind cannot achieve) and thereby taking control of the body. For example, if you could interpret your dreams and visions and apply it in your everyday life, you are in charge of your body. You will live a good and serene life, devoid of much stress.

However, if you live a carnal life – as a physical mind – you will wander about, suffer so much in body, and live a confused and directionless life.

CHAPTER 42– THE MIND MUST BOW TO THE SPIRIT

Those that rejected the ways of the Spiritual Mind – Joseph – had to come back. The senses, intellect, memory, conscience that previously rejected the message of the Spirit had to return when the latter conquered the Mind.

Put differently, when the spiritual mind conquered the physical mind, all other attributes of the Mind (senses, intellect, conscience, etc.) were also subdued and had to follow through. They suddenly realized themselves and had to turn back to the Spirit.

CHAPTERS 43 AND 44— THE MIND MUST BOW TO THE SPIRIT

Reference: Chapter 42

CHAPTERS 45 TO 50— BODY, MIND AND SPIRIT BECOME ONE

The Mind has realized himself as the Spirit. There is now a unification of Mind, Body and Spirit. Put in another way, the mind has attained perfection or self-realization.

Recall that Jacob and Joseph are minds that followed the Spirit – Chapter 28 and 37. Joseph's brothers are Minds that followed the body, Chapter 37. Pharaoh is the King of the body.

All these characters are now united as one.

EXODUS

CHAPTER 1– END OF AN AGE

Verse 1 The Iron Age has emerged and the spiritual minds had gone back to carnality and gross materialism – "Jacob and his sons (*spiritual minds*) went down to Egypt (*body/carnality*)"– TLB.

Take note that Hebrew/Jews represent spiritual minds. Midwives represent Neutral Mind which acts as moderator between the Hebrews (spiritual minds) and the Egyptians (physical minds). The mind in this neutral stage can also be described as Intellect. In Igbo Language, it is referred to as *Mkpoko Echiche*, meaning to collate and sieve what the Mind has created.

Therefore, the Mind in its neutral stage performs dual roles. It can apply its agents (senses, intellect, memory, conscience and bodies) to follow the Spirit, and thus becomes a spiritual mind. Alternatively, it could also deploy these agents to follow the body and hence becomes a physical mind. And so there is a constant battle raging between these two groups. This conflict in a person was aptly captured by Saint Paul in his letter to the people of Galatia, Chapter 5:16-26.

This was exactly the drama that was reported from verses 8 to 18 of Chapter one of Exodus.

Verse 19 those in the Spirit understand quickly and they come forth with spiritual messages (*babies*). Remember that each time the High Priest or Herod sends his aides to investigate Jesus' sermons, they would end up being convinced by Him.

CHAPTER 2 – EMERGENCE OF MOSES AS A MESSIAH; AND THE STORY OF CREATION

Verse 1–10 *Creation* (How the body was formed): Pharaoh's daughter represents physical Intellect. Anything the mind creates is a daughter (She). Wisdom, for example is addressed as She. Hebrew's son symbolizes the spiritual mind. The physical intellect longs for the spiritual Wisdom/Intelligence/Knowledge (Moses)– verses 5, 6.

The baby's sister (verse 4) stands for spiritual intellect whereas the Mother (verse 8) symbolizes physical body which will take custody of the Spirit.

In the drama of Creation, the spiritual intellect stand in the place of Fire and the physical intellect replaces

Water. Hence both agreed to entrust the Spirit unto the body wherein it will carry out its activities on earth (verse 7).

Verse 11-12 Moses is the Messiah: Moses has realized himself as the Messiah. He has conquered his mind and is now spiritual. He has attained 400,000 years of consciousness and has started "killing" the minds and thoughts that are carnal, mundane and materialistic through his messages.

Verse 13-15 Moses is rejected because nobody could understand His spiritual messages.

Verse 16-22 Moses' marital life: He was married with children

Verse 23-25 He has a burning desire to save mankind through his messages.

CHAPTER 3– MOSES RECEIVES MANDATE FROM THE SUPREME SPIRIT

Full consciousness and awareness has now finally dawned on Moses.

Verse 2-5 The bush refers to dirt and carnality in the Mind. *"A Flame of Fire in a bush/Burning bush"* means, the Spirit consumed the dirt in the Mind. The Mind and Spirit thus became one.

Shoe refers to attachment in the physical whereas holy place means spiritual awareness. Moses realized that at his level of consciousness, he doesn't need any physical attachment or support that would help him in his spiritual mission.

Verse 6 I am *Mmuo, Mmuo-Okike, Mmuo-Ozi*. This is the Trinity.

Verse 7-10 Moses is determined to bring the Good News of Salvation to Mankind. "*To deliver them from Egyptians*" means to salvage them from carnality, worldliness and gross materialism; to teach them that they are not physical body but Spirit. This is the Mission of every True Messiah.

When it is recorded that '*the Lord said to Moses,*' always bear in mind that it is Moses talking to himself, i.e. Moses (the Spirit) and the mind are conversing. Recall that Moses is the incarnate of the Supreme Spirit. There is no more duality. Both (Supreme Spirit and Messiah) have become one.

Verse 11-13 Doubts (self-doubt) welled up in him, but he encouraged himself. The mind was scared of the assignment. But the Spirit assured him It will be with him.

Verse 14-22 Moses (the Spirit) and the mind are conversing. The mind was relating what the Spirit ministered unto it – what the mind and body will do. "*The Sovereign God…I AM has sent me!*" (TLB) Moses made this statement. He projected this scene from himself because he is the Spirit – '*I am who I am,*' i.e. '*Mmuo a bu Mmuo;*' '*I and My Father are one.*'

- *Commentaries*

Verse 18 *"….journey into the desert…"* means, to be in the mind; thinking of what to do to save the people from worldliness and carnality.

Verse 20 *"….miracles of God…"* refer to earthquakes, volcanoes, typhoons that will commence at the appearance of Rainbow Cross in the sky. These happenings will culminate seven days to the beginning of the Three Days of Darkness.

Verse 21-22 These are the benefits that will accrue to the Apostles and followers of Moses in the course of his mission at End-Time; personal effects they will use as they pass over to the Golden Age.

CHAPTER 4– MOSES LACKS COURAGE

Verse 1-5 Moses' (Mind) is disturbed. He is restless. He has doubts and fears. The Spirit advises he should allow his mind to be straight – that his mind and Spirit become one. *Rod* refers to straight or righteous mind. Serpent is mind that is not right with the Spirit.

Verse 5 "Do that and they will believe you – TLB," means 'straighten your mind or stand at right with the Spirit and people will believe your message of Salvation.'

Verse 6-9 The Spirit warns Moses to desist from running away from the mission. Indeed, Moses doubts the Spirit. It therefore, advises Moses to put back those problems (fears, doubts, discouragement etc.) unto the

Spirit. That once he puts those problems away, people will believe him.

Verse 6 Being infected with small pox, chicken pox and leprosy in visions and dreams is a sign of disobedience to God's commandment. The person is thereby warned. However, if the person becomes unrepentant or recalcitrant, the disease comes upon him in real life.

Verse 9 "*….then take water from the Nile River and pour it upon dry land, and it will turn to blood*"– TLB. Water here means trouble or worries; blood symbolizes power and dry land, heart. Therefore, if Moses evacuates his heart of all his worries, power will come and they will believe him.

Verse 10-17 Moses continued to protest within himself but assured himself of the assistance of Aaron – who is more eloquent and outspoken.

Verse 18-23 '*Moses returned back to Egypt*'– Moses awakened from sleep and came back to his physical body. Recall that all these experiences were in visions, not real life.

Verse 24-26 Zipporah encourages Moses to go ahead with the mission. Sharp stone or a flint knife (KJV) means sharp heart. "*What a blood-smeared husband you've turned out to be*" (TLB) means, "You are a powerful husband to me because you did not die."

Verse 27-31 This is a revelation/vision. Moses and Aaron did not physically go to Pharaoh or Egypt. Rather the Spiritual mind (represented by Moses and Aaron) are persuading the physical minds (represented by Pharaoh and Egyptians, i.e. mankind) to join them.

CHAPTER 5– MANKIND REJECTS THE MESSAGE OF MOSES

Verse 1-3 Moses advises people to abandon the life of carnality and gross materialism; and begin to think about the Spirit. Wilderness or desert refers to Mind; thinking or pondering.

Verse 4-21 But carnality, worldliness and love for material things have assumed an unprecedented dimension. People are dead and indifferent to spiritual matters. They are busy accumulating physical and perishable articles; giving no heed to the teachings of the Messiah.

Verse 22-23 Moses is disappointed.

CHAPTER 6– MOSES BATTLES IN HIS MIND

Verse 1 But difficulties in the life of these people will now compel them to seek the Messiah. These carnal people are forced to seek spiritual messages.

Verse 2-8 To those who really love the Lord – the seekers and few genuine Christians holding church titles and positions – the Spirit reiterates his promises through Moses: to help them realize themselves as Spirit.

Verse 9 Moses reminded them of those promises, but mankind still doubted because of the confusion and suffering in the world. A few people had arisen in the past and had claimed to be Messiahs. At long last, they failed their gullible followers because they were false teachers and prophets. Hence, mankind is confused, disenchanted and dispirited. Consequently, they can no longer listen to Moses, the Messiah.

Verse 10-12 Mankind's spiritual lethargy and indifference has really worn Moses out. He lamented that the few ones who are spiritually minded (e.g. pastors, priests and prophets) could not believe his messages, how much less the carnally minded. So he protested going out any more to talk to them.

Verse 13 But Moses cannot keep quiet for too long. He has a burning desire to go out and speak in order to deliver mankind from imminent disaster. He is compelled by his mandate to go out with Aaron and continue to teach the message of Salvation to the people.

CHAPTER 7– FALSE TEACHERS CHALLENGE MOSES/ MANKIND REMAINS

- **Unrepentant**

Verse 1-7 Moses is determined to join forces with Aaron to speak to the people. If they refuse to hear, they will suffer terribly and will be forced to seek Moses.

Verse 8-10 The mission is on but the people are still unyielding, adamant and unrepentant. Moses delivers his messages through Aaron's beautiful and eloquent speech. *Rod* represents spiritual or straight mind; *serpent* refers to different manners and styles of teachings adopted by Aaron.

Verse 11 simultaneously, the false teachers and prophets (carnal people or Egyptian magicians) exhibited their own false teachings. They argued with Moses and Aaron.

Verse 12 But Aaron's teachings overshadowed and proved more superior to theirs.

Verse 13-14 Nevertheless the people remained adamant.

Verse 15 Moses is determined to continue to teach the people in his righteousness (i.e. "*holding in your hand the rod that turned into a serpent*") His message still remained: abandon carnal life and begin "to think" (wilderness) about spiritual matters.

Verse 17-18 When the message hits them, they will be shaken. The message will uproot their age-long carnal and false beliefs. Consequently, they will begin to reject those false teachings in their churches and temples. River here refers to trouble (their false beliefs and teachings). Fish means people; and blood stand for power that uproots those false beliefs.

Verse 19-20 The message of Moses spread in all nooks and crannies of the land.

Verse 22 The false teachers (priests and pastors) also continued to give out their own deceitful teachings to counter the messages of Moses. This made their followers more unrepentant.

Verse 24 Nevertheless, Moses' messages overwhelmed theirs. They couldn't challenge Him. As a result, they receded and started hiding their own teachings.

CHAPTERS 8, 9, 10 AND 11– HARDSHIP HAS SET IN

Continued refusal to hearken to the messages of Moses resulted in untold sufferings and hardship to people – earthquakes, volcanoes, typhoon, diseases, poverty, death, bad leadership, moral depravity, etc (i.e. *the plagues*). Read *Matthew 24*– Signs of the End-Time as predicted by Jesus Christ of Nazareth.

Chapter 10:4-23 *Three Days of Darkness:* This is the day (the Anger) of the Lord – *Amos 5:18-20*. Moses is about to bring the age to a close. But mankind still remained recalcitrant and unyielding to his message.

CHAPTER 12– THREE DAYS OF DARKNESS: PASSING OVER TO THE GOLDEN AGE

The inevitable three days of darkness took place. This is a time the Supreme Spirit releases His Anger and the whole world shakes. The spiritual minds will be protected from all the problems and sufferings that will arise then.

The nights will be utterly cold; the wind will howl and roar. Then will come lightning, earthquakes, thunderbolts and stars. Heavenly bodies will be disturbed and become restless. There will be no light, but total darkness. Utter darkness will envelop the entire earth. This will come suddenly like a flash.

The angels of God who are the executioners of this work are standing ready with swords. They will take special care to annihilate all those who mock the Messiah; and would not believe his messages. After marking the servants of God with a seal on their foreheads, then, God will release His Angels whom he had given the power to damage the earth – *Revelation 7:2, 3.*

After the three days of darkness or the great "chastisement" are over, there will be no more evil person left. The evil ones will be annihilated. Seventy-five percent of humanity will be destroyed – Revelation 9:18. Every other person left on earth will have faith in God with all their hearts. The devastation will be astonishingly great, but the earth will be purified.

The Sun will shine again and it will be as spring time. All will be fair and beautiful. The Holy angels will descend from heaven and spread the Spirit of Peace over the earth and the righteous will be able to start life anew. This is what it means to pass over to the Golden Age.

Verse 6-13 *Unleavened bread* refers to the true message of the Messiah. *Lambs* are humble and meek people, following the ways of the Spirit. When the lambs are *roasted*, it means these people have completely surrendered to the Spirit. *Blood* means power arising from awareness of the Spirit. *Blood on the door posts* refer to the Seal of God. *Yeast* is false message from false teachers. *Yeast-less* bread is Truth Unblemished; true message as taught by the True Messiah.

Verse 29 "*…that night, at midnight, the Lord killed all the first born sons in the land of Egypt…*"TLB. Firstborn of the Egyptians refers to firstborn of the body which is Mind. Before the body was created, there was Mind. Killing the firstborn sons means that the carnally-minded people were destroyed.

Verse 40 "*The sons of Jacob and their descendants had lived in Egypt 430 years, and it was on the last day of the 430ᵗʰ year that all of Jehovah's people left the land*" Salvation and self-realization takes place exactly at 400,000 years (not 430 years) of consciousness. The Spirit spends 400,000 years in the human body before it leaves to unite with the Supreme Spirit i.e. eternal life. It is always people that had clocked 400,000 years that understand the Messiah and therefore cross over to the Golden Age.

Verse 43 "*….no foreigners shall eat the roasted lamb…*" Ordinary members only believe in the Spirit. They do not know Him. Besides, they do not believe in the Messiah but are merely following him for sake of miracles. Therefore, they have not completely surrendered to the Spirit.

Verse 48 If they are to be passed over to the Promised Land, they must purify (*circumcise*) their hearts.

CHAPTER 13– THE MIND NOW FOLLOWS THE SPIRIT (MANKIND NOW THINKS ABOUT SPIRITUAL MATTERS)

On the third day, a feeling of immeasurable gratitude will possess the hearts of those who survive this terrible and horrible ordeal. And upon the return of sunlight, they will kneel down immediately and give thanks to the Supreme Spirit for their protection.

Verse 1 The mind that followed the Spirit (firstborn) should worship the Lord. They belong to Him. *Israelele* means nations or peoples. It does not refer to a particular country or nation. The nation, called by '*Israel*' today only adopted it as a name.

Verse 17 At last the mind has followed the Spirit.

Verse 18 The road to eternal life is not rosy nor comfortable. It is a narrow road. We must work out our Salvation with trembling and fear.

Verse 19 Moses took the remains of the teachings of past prophets (e.g. Joseph) even though they were no longer alive. Those messages had helped the people abandon carnal life.

Verse 21 – the guiding Light of the message, in the journey to eternal life.

CHAPTER 14 – PHYSICAL HARDSHIP FOLLOWS LIFE IN THE SPIRIT

Whenever the mind begins to follow the Spirit i.e. when a person begins to place the things of the Spirit first, all the physical attractions of life begin to give way.

Naturally, the mind will cry, lament and complain, because the body is not used to "thinking about spiritual things" (i.e. *life in the wilderness).*

Verse 11-14 Difficulties arising from the practice of the true knowledge of the Spirit has started. Obviously, when a person begins to worship God in truth and spirit, but still struggles with earthly problems, friends, relatives and neighbours (who are still carnal and mundane) will taunt and abuse him. And because the person is still in the flesh, pressures will definitely set in. He may begin to question God, wondering whether there is any benefit in serving Him.

Red Sea signifies great and enormous trouble that faced the Apostles of Moses i.e. those following the messages of the Spirit.

Verse 15-31 *Rod* represents straight Mind or righteous Mind of Moses. "*Use your rod – hold it out over the water, and the sea will open up a path before you, and all the people of Israel shall walk through on dry ground*" TLB. Moses used his message to resolve the trouble his Apostles faced. He mediated in the case between them and their contenders and dispersed the latter. And the problems that confronted his Apostles later came upon their contenders.

CHAPTER 15– PHYSICAL HARDSHIP CONTINUES

Verse 1-21 Moses' Apostles worshipped the Spirit as these problems are solved.

Verse 22 "….*without water…*" means they went about their activities free of trouble.

Verse 23 "….*bitter water…*" signifies sudden trouble

Verse 24 "Must we die in this trouble"– TLB

Verse 25 '*Tree*' here refers to true message: revelation of hope concerning their situation. The problem was solved (*water became sweet*) by the message of hope received.

CHAPTER 16– PHYSICAL HARDSHIP DEEPENS BUT SPIRITUAL KNOWLEDGE SUFFICES

Verse 1-2 Problems are solved one after another. People who abandon the body (carnality) feel that things will continue to be rosy. But problems kept rearing their heads from time to time. As a result, they never cease complaining.

Verses 3, 4 People are no longer satisfied with spiritual food. They yearn for physical food.

Verse 6-15 *Manna* is spiritual knowledge.

Verse 16 The spiritual message should be taken in piecemeal – take as much as you can *digest* (comprehend, practice).

Verse 19-24 Moses warned on the dangers of carrying the message without understanding. Such attempt will result in interpersonal conflict, agitation and confrontation. Such a person would eventually jettison the message.

Verse 25-30 *Six days* refer to the six created bodies whereas seventh day is the seventh body wherein the mind will follow the Spirit or the person would have realized himself as Spirit.

Verse 26 *"Gather the food for six days, but the seventh is a Sabbath, and there will be none there for you on that day* – TLB

Verse 29 *"Don't they realize that I am giving them twice as much on the sixth day, so that there will be enough for two days? For the Lord has given you the seventh day as a day of Sabbath rest; stay in your tents and don't go out to pick up food from the ground that day"* TLB.

It is in the human body (sixth body) that we need to acquire as much spiritual knowledge that will enable us attain Salvation or self-realization (seventh body).

Verse 32-34 The message should be passed on from generation to generation.

Verse 35 They lived with the message for 400,000 years until they realized themselves as spirit.

CHAPTER 17– MOSES PROVOKED BY PEOPLES' IMPATIENCE

Verse 1-4 Peoples' material expectations are not met. They still complain. Frustrated, they now invite disaster. They want to die because they are tired of this life. Economic, domestic and political pressures are too much resulting to impatience among the followers. They are no longer sustained by their faith and conviction in the message. They want to opt out and go back to the world (carnality).

The Book of Genesis, Chapter 19:26 recorded that *Lot's wife looked back…and became a pillar of salt* i.e. she went back to carnality and was destroyed alongside other evil people. Jesus also counseled His disciples on the problems at the end of the world in the Book of Matthew 24; but assured them in verse 13 that *"….those who endure to the end shall be saved."*

Verse 5-7 The people provoked Moses by their impatience. Out of anger in his heart, he talked to them before his Apostles (elders of Israel). *Rock* here refers to strong heart (of Moses).

'Strike the rock with your rod, and water will come pouring out'– means that Moses counseled them angrily.

Verse 8-9 Moses sent Joshua (his chief Apostle) to go and talk to certain groups. He (Moses) assured him of his support.

Verse 10 *Fight against the Amalekites* refers to the battle of the believers and non-believers during the mission of Moses. It is the battle of the Spirit, Mind and Body. Joshua, Aaron and Hur were active supporters of the mission of Moses.

Verse 11, 12 They encouraged Moses to be steadfast – by developing strong heart.

CHAPTER 18- MOSES UNITES WITH HIS FAMILY

Verse 1-12 Pressures emanating from the mission mounted. Moses had sent his family – wife and two sons – away to stay with his father-in-law, Jethro. Here they were united again.

Verse 13-26 Jethro counsels Moses on administrative strategies.

CHAPTER 19- MOSES GIVES THE LAWS

Verse 12 Boundary lines refer to limits or Laws; do's and don'ts; rules and regulations.

CHAPTER 20- MOSES' TEN COMMANDMENTS

Verse 5 Exceptions to this Law are images of the Messiah and Holy Mothers.

Verse 11 *Sabbath Day*: Concerning the last/sixth created body (human), Moon (*Onwa*) representing the female, was the first planet to appear after having completed the first 200,000 years. This was followed by Sun, representing the male, which appeared at the end of the next 200,000 years i.e. the human body clocking altogether 400,000 years at the end of the First Creation.

At this point, the Spirit, Mind and Body became one i.e. Man attained self-realization or self-consciousness; and then rested. This was the *seventh body, seventh day or Sabbath Day.*

Verses 18, 19 Mankind has recently emerged from the three days of darkness; and are gratefully scared of what happened. Consequently, they have completely surrendered to Moses with unflinching and unalloyed obedience and loyalty.

Verse 24-26 Altar and Stone refer to heart; Undiluted, Unblemished pure heart.

CHAPTER 21-27– MOSES' OTHER LAWS

'*Building altars*' means building the hearts of men.

CHAPTER 28-31– WORSHIP (SERVICE) RULES AND REGULATIONS

CHAPTER 32– SIN OF DISOBEDIENCE SETS IN

Verse 1 '*Went to the mountain or hill*' means being in the Spirit; meditating; thinking about the Spirit.

'*Golden Calf*'– Aaron lured a group of people out of the congregation. He created a faction which worshipped Materialism. Golden Calf represents material and physical things people worship due to ignorance of the true teachings of God.

At the end of age when Moses had returned to become one with the Supreme Spirit, the World resorted to worshipping materialism.

In spiritual context, Aaron could also represent Mind.

CHAPTER 33-34- MOSES RECEIVES REVELATIONS FROM THE SUPREME SPIRIT

CHAPTER 35-40— MORE SERVICE RULES AND REGULATIONS

Ark refers to heart. *Covenants* are teachings or Laws of the Spirit. *Covenant Box* symbolizes the heart where the teachings are stored or saved. *Tabernacle* is body; *temple* also stands for body.

NUMBERS

CHAPTER 1-4- CENSUS FOR RESPONSIBILITY

Census (numbering) was conducted for the purpose of assignment of responsibilities and duties to members of the mission as follows–

1. To go to war: these are the members that conduct seminars, crusades and evangelism for the purpose of winning converts. The enemies of the Israelites (spiritual minds) are the carnal, mundane and the physically-minded people. When it is said that the Israelites destroyed their enemies, it means that they were won over or converted to their own congregation; or defeated in arguments or debates. It is not a physical battle or war. Nobody died physically.

2. To work and care for the Tabernacle: These are the medical and welfare corps. They are

responsible for the health and physical needs of the members.

3. To care for the Ark.

CHAPTER 5-10- MORE SERVICE RULES AND REGULATIONS

Reference: Exodus 28-31, 35-40

CHAPTER 11- THE PEOPLE STILL COMPLAIN OF MISFORTUNES

The people are no longer satisfied with the spiritual teachings of Moses because their physical circumstances are getting worse as days pass. They want to go back to the world in order to be able to meet their economic needs.

Nevertheless, they were overwhelmed and calmed by the power in the teachings of Moses – *verses1, 32, 33*. The negativity of their mind was killed to enable them accept the Spirit.

Fire of the Lord represents the power of the Spirit. *Quail* is *Manna* which stands for the spiritual messages.

CHAPTER 12- MIRIAM AND AARON REBEL AGAINST MOSES

Both became jealous of Moses. Miriam was however, warned (*attack of leprosy*) by God.

CHAPTER 13 AND 14- PEOPLE LOSES CONFIDENCE IN SALVATION

In view of the lust and desire for carnal things, Salvation, Self-realization and Eternal Life are fast becoming an illusion and delusion for the people. They have lost confidence in achieving self-consciousness. They want to go back to carnality (*Egypt*).

Chapter 14:6-10 But Caleb and Joshua convinced them of the feasibility of achieving eternal life (Promised Land). The *twelve (12)* spies sent out represent the Trinity (12=1+2=3)– Spirit, Mind and Body. It is the Trinity that reveals or spies out journey to eternal life i.e. the possibility of a person realizing himself as Spirit.

Chapter 14:37 The doubters and instigators (*other ten spies*) had their negative minds 'killed' through the messages of the Spirit.

Chapter 14:44-45 Owing to the people's ill-preparedness, their enemies defeated them in a debate.

CHAPTER 15- SERVICE RULES AND REGULATIONS

CHAPTER 16- GROUP REBELS AGAINST MOSES

A group of followers who have been very close to Moses, but felt they have learnt quite a lot, sponsored an insurrection to challenge Moses' spiritual authority over them.

Moses invited them for a contest and debate (verse 16-20). They were defeated (verse 31-33) and the little authority they presumed they had was taken away from them (verse 36-38). From that day on, people realized that one had to be deep-rooted in the message before claiming any spiritual authority.

CHAPTER 17- CHOOSING THE GROUP LEADER

Verse 1-5 Since jealous and rivalry have crept in among the followers concerning who should command authority, Moses received a revelation (vision) on how such a group leader should emerge.

Verse 8 Aaron was eventually chosen by the Spirit as the most matured of all the Apostles. The message is very well deep-rooted in him and he understands the Messiah better than others. This exercise did not happen physically. *"Aaron's rod"* means straight or righteous mind. *"…budded and was blossoming, and had ripe almonds…"* means his understanding of the message is much more matured, deep-rooted and brilliant.

Recall a similar scenario during Jesus' time. He asked his disciples who he was: Peter answered,

> *"The Christ, the Messiah, the Son of the Living God. And Jesus said, "God has blessed you, Simon, son of Jonah, for my Father in heaven has personally revealed this to you – this is not from any human source. You are Peter, a Stone; and upon this rock I will build my Church; and the powers of hell shall not prevail*

> *against it. And I will give you the keys*
> *of the Kingdom of Heaven; whatever*
> *doors you lock on earth shall be locked in*
> *heaven; and whatever doors you open on*
> *earth shall be opened in heaven!"*– TLB,
> Matthew 16:15-19

This event conferred the group leadership on Peter.

CHAPTERS 18 AND 19- SERVICE RULES AND REGULATIONS

CHAPTER 20- THE PEOPLE MOCK GOD

Verse 2-5 Prevalent difficult circumstances have continued to stare the people in the face resulting in persistent loss of hope and faith in the journey to eternal life. People have therefore resorted to mocking and daring God. They regretted; and cursed Moses for bringing them out of their previous comfortable but carnal life (Egypt). In fact they are courting the Anger of the Spirit.

Verse 6-11 Moses rebuked them vehemently and uncontrollably. "*...and struck the rock twice..."* Rock means strong heart– a heart that follows the Spirit.

Verse 12 The Spirit and Mind are in conflict. Moses wondered if his action would not tantamount to his not trusting the Spirit any longer. It is similar to what happened on the Cross of Calvary, wherein Jesus cried, "*...my Lord, my Lord, why has thou forsaken me."*

Verse 14-22 Moses asked for a favor from a certain influential person but was turned down.

Verse 23-29 Aaron died and was replaced by his son, Eliezer.

CHAPTER 21– THE PEOPLE MURMUR AGAINST GOD

Verse 4-6 The mind of the people has drifted away from following the Spirit; and has gone back to carnality (body). They are disappointed because of unfulfilled life expectations. Indeed the road to eternal life is very rough and uncomfortable. All their expectations to make it materially were not fulfilled. So they were discouraged, and then were backslidden i.e. went back to the world.

Consequently, they started experiencing all those evils associated with physical and material things; they became greatly troubled in the mind; sickness arose; stress increased; anxiety and high blood pressure were aggravated in their lives. People were terribly agitated. Simply put, their mind brought negativity, troubles and problems.

Recall that Snake stands for mind. "*That snake bit them*" means their minds were warped in morbid pondering giving rise to negativity, gross materialism and carnality as aforementioned.

Verse 7-9 "Straighten your mind; return back to the Spirit. Let your mind follow the Spirit, and all worries will vanish."

CHAPTER 22-24- AN UNBELIEVER OBSTRUCTS THE PEOPLE OF MOSES

Chapter 22 If you are following the Spirit, be watchful. Observe when He changes instructions. Donkey here represents Mind. A similar case is that of Prophet Jonah's mission to the city of Nineveh.

CHAPTER 25- THE PEOPLE SIN AGAIN

CHAPTER 26- ANOTHER CENSUS TAKES PLACE

CHAPTER 27- APPOINTMENT OF JOSHUA

Joshua is appointed to continue to teach the people; and prepare them for eternal life, if and when Moses, the Messiah passes on.

CHAPTER 28-30- MORE SERVICE RULES AND REGULATIONS

CHAPTER 31- NEGATIVE MINDS DESTROYED

See Chapter 1-4

CHAPTER 32-36- (NO SPIRITUAL VALUE TO MAN)

DEUTERONOMY

The Book of Deuteronomy consists of a series of farewell messages by Moses. They are addressed to the very few people who are destined for Salvation. These Laws can be understood the way they are.

"Two tablets of the Law" refer to two chambers of the heart – the negative and positive part of the heart.

"Door posts of your house" are the lips and tongues of your body, i.e. 'let the laws of God be in your lips and mouth always and at all times.

CHAPTER 28, 29 AND 30 – LAWS OF THE SPIRIT/GOD'S COVENANTS WITH MANKIND

The commandments are the Laws of Creation; not Church laws.

How does one obey these Laws (of Creation):

1. Know the Spirit, i.e. by experiencing the Spirit
2. Obeying the Ten Commandments – Exodus 20

CHAPTER 31-33– MOSES VALEDICTORY SPEECHES

Chapter 31 Moses admonishes and encourages his Apostles knowing full well that his days are drawing near.

Chapter 32 He worships the Spirit in view of all the great miracles He has done through him (Moses).

Chapter 33 Moses empowers and blesses them.

CHAPTER 34 – MOSES' DEATH AND RESURRECTION

Verse 6 "*…but no man knoweth of his sepulcher unto this day*"– KJV. Moses died and was buried, but his '*body*' was not found in the sepulcher. The body referred to here is not his physical body but his '*Mind*' body, indicating therefore that he was resurrected. His Mind has become One with the Spirit.

A similar incident happened in the case of Jesus Christ of Nazareth as recorded in John 20:1, 2 (KJV)

> "*The first day of the week cometh Mary Magdalene early, when it was yet dark, unto the sepulcher, and seeth the stone taken away from the sepulcher. Then she runneth, and cometh to Simon Peter, and to other disciple, whom Jesus loved, and said unto them, 'They have taken the*

> *Lord out of the sepulcher, and we know*
> *not where they have laid him"*

Jesus had resurrected. Indeed, resurrection is the evidence of a True Messiah.

JOSHUA

After the death of Moses, Joshua was anointed to carry on with the Mission of Moses. It was he who eventually led mankind (the Apostles) into eternal life, Salvation or Self-awareness i.e. the Promised Land.

CHAPTER 1– JOSHUA TAKES OVER

Joshua takes over; and encourages his people to be prepared to endure a few problems; and thereafter earn their Salvation.

Jesus encouraged his disciples, *"But those enduring to the end shall be saved."*– TLB Matthew 24:13

CHAPTER 2– THE SPIRIT ASSURES THEM OF ETERNAL LIFE

The Spirit reveals to them that Salvation is attainable. Therefore they should not be fainthearted.

CHAPTERS 3 AND 4– A LITTLE MORE HURDLES TO CROSS

River Jordan, just like Red Sea, represents a great trouble facing the Apostles of Moses.

Chapter 3:3 *"When you see the Priests carrying the Ark of God, follow them. You have never before seen where we are going now, so they will guide you…"* Recall that Ark of God means Heart of God. The people were encouraged to cultivate the kind of heart their spiritual leaders possess. For that is the only way they can cross the hurdle; and come out of the troubles facing them, unscathed.

CHAPTER 5– JOSHUA RECEIVES MESSAGES OF ASSURANCE

Verse 2 *"….Make the sharp knives, and circumcise again the children of Israel."* Recall that sharp or flint knives represent Sharp Heart. The members are to circumcise their hearts – make their heart stronger and sharper in understanding the teachings of the Spirit towards their journey to eternal life.

Verse 13-15 Joshua was assured of victory but was advised, like his Master Moses, not to rely on any physical attachment he presumes would assist in his Missio Exodus 3:5

CHAPTER 6– THE PEOPLE FACES A POWERFUL/STRONG FALSEHOOD

Jericho represents a very strong mind that follows the body – mind suffused with sordid carnality and gross materialism. The wall of Jericho stands for Falsehood that was built around the mind. Sound of the trumpets is the true message of the Spirit.

Verse 20 "*So the people shouted when the priests blew with the trumpets….the wall fell down…*"

The Spirit, through the true teachings/messages pulled down the falsehood that was built around the carnal mind. The message then penetrated the minds; and converts were made.

CHAPTERS 7- 12- DEFEATS AND CONQUESTS OF THE PEOPLE

Occasionally, the Apostles of Moses were defeated in debates, arguments and seminars. But oftentimes, they would win converts over to their mission.

CHAPTERS 13- 22- THE APOSTLES HAVE ATTAINED SALVATION

Dividing the land, assigning of land or settlements of the tribes of Israel refer to self-realization, self-awareness or consciousness. The Apostles have finally realized themselves as spirits.

CHAPTERS 23- 24- JOSHUA'S LAST DAYS

Joshua declared his valedictory speech; encouraging his people to be very courageous in keeping and doing all that is written in the Laws brought by Moses….

THE TEACHINGS
OF JESUS

MATTHEW

CHAPTER 1- VIRGIN BIRTH OF JESUS CHRIST

Verse 18–25 Everybody and all human beings are conceived by the Supreme Spirit (*Holy Spirit*). There cannot, therefore be any conception without the power of the Spirit.

But actual conception takes place spiritually within the womb of the woman. The female gamete (female reproductive organ) consists of both male and female natures. And so, even without the introduction of male sperm, the female gamete can on its own bring about fertilization consequent upon the meeting of the male and female natures resident therein; and further development of the fetus.

It should be noted that this circumstance is peculiar to unique and special children such as Messiahs; some prophets and even scientific discoverers. It is a mystery in creation that does not always occur; and for all births.

Concerning births (other than the Messiah's), a man will physically introduce sperm, through sexual intercourse into the womb of the woman, for purposes of subsequent confirmation.

Against this backdrop, therefore, there was no biological conception in the case of Jesus; rather an entrance of the Spirit. The Spirit entered the womb of Mary and developed the specific body, It wanted to use for the work of Redemption. At annunciation of the birth of Jesus by the Angel, the entrance or the so-called conception had already taken place in the Spirit before it manifested in the physical. *There was no physical contact with a man.*

Therefore, the physical body of the Messiah can never be conceived through the process of the physical union of man and woman. The physical birth of Jesus was not a biological conception but a product of an arrangement of the Supreme Spirit. Put differently, sexual intercourse between a man and a woman cannot give rise to the birth of the physical body of a Messiah.

So what happened? When the female physical body the Supreme Spirit wants to use is ready, it will descend onto it. The Virginity of Mary, the Mother of Jesus was not a carnal one, but derives from a *Purity of Heart and Right Standing* with the Supreme Spirit. The Messiah cannot be contained in the womb of a woman nor be delivered through her genitals.

Besides, the physical body does not make the Messiah. He is the incarnate of the Supreme Being. This is purely spiritual. Nevertheless, his physical body obeyed all the laws regulating the physical processes of Creation.

And so that Jesus was born of a Virgin means that He came with all the attributes of *Perfection, Truth Unblemished, Love, Righteousness, Peace and Joy.*

CHAPTER 2– JESUS RECEIVES MANDATE AS THE MESSIAH

Verse 1–12 Jesus related this '*spiritual experience*' to his Apostles. The incident never occurred physically. It was a revelation. The three '*Wise men or Astrologers*' from the East are the immediate three past incarnations of Jesus namely Lot, Melchizedek and Moses.

Recall the words of Moses in Deuteronomy 18:15, 18, "*Instead, he will raise up for you a Prophet like Me, an Israeli, a man to whom you must listen and whom you must obey…I will raise up from among them a Prophet, and he shall be my spokesman to the people.*" TLB

That God will raise a prophet like me simply means that Moses will come again. Prophet "like me" referred to here does not mean the physical body and name of Moses. "Like me" means that the same Spirit that spoke in the body and with the name of Moses, will come again, as the Messiah.

Prophet Isaiah prophesied that the new name of the Messiah should be called Immanuel – Isaiah 7:14, *"All right then, the Lord himself will choose the Sign, i.e. a child shall be born to a Virgin. And she shall call him Immanuel – meaning God is with us."* TLB

Recall also that Moses had told his people then, that when he returns, he would be called by a new name. That new name was derived from *"among them"*, which is a synonym for the phrase, *"With us"*– the meaning of Immanuel (God is with us).

When the Messiah was born, he was named *Jesus*. The Hebrew equivalent of the Greek name *Iesous* or Jesus is *Yehoshua* meaning *God is our Salvation (God is with us* – to save us*)*.

Verse 11 *Gold, Frankincense and Myrrh* are cherished gifts obtainable in that part of the world at that time. Niike na Ebube Dara Ndu was given *"ofo"*– (a symbol of authority in Igbo tradition) – by His three immediate past incarnations i.e. Melchizedek, Moses and Jesus.

The three different gifts, representing messianic power and mandate, given to Jesus as recorded in this chapter suggest that his messages will be in piecemeal; yet complete. This perhaps explains why some mystics describe Him as a Semi-Avatar.

Verse 13–23 *"Get up and flee to Egypt…"* While Jesus was still in the body – *Egypt* (i.e. his pre-mission period) he has already assumed self-consciousness. Afterwards, he came back to his mission during which his Mind

(*King Herod*) would have been calmed (*killed or died*). *Egypt* represents body, flesh or physical activities. *King Herod* stands for Mind.

As an instance, Dara Ndu knew about his spiritual awareness or self-realization *ab initio.* But as he was growing up, he did all sorts of jobs, engaged in all kinds of businesses. At the appropriate time, he declared his mission and since then, has been occupied only with the teachings of the message of the Spirit.

CHAPTER 3– JOHN THE BAPTIST– FORERUNNER OF JESUS

Verse 1–6 Shortly before the Messiah emerges, there is always a Prophet who, acting as a fore-runner, announces the coming of the Savior. His mission is simply to prepare the minds of mankind to be ripened enough to receive the True one – the Messiah.

Examples of such prophets and the contemporary Messiahs are as follows:

	Prophets	*The Messiah*
1	Abraham	Melchizedek
2	Elijah	Moses
3	John the Baptist	Jesus
4	Guru Maharaj Ji	Dara Ndu

Verse 7–17 Baptism means spiritual power; spiritual anointing from a higher being to a human being. Baptism means impartation or giving of power to do the work of God. Every Messiah gives power to certain

prophets to go ahead of Him and prepare the way. The greatest in the lineage were Elijah and John the Baptist.

When the Messiah emerges, He collects the power back. This is what happened between Jesus and John the Baptist in this chapter. Recall the visits between Elizabeth and Mary, the mother of Jesus, after the Annunciation. The Bible recorded that as soon as Mary greeted Elizabeth, the baby in the womb of the latter jumped up for joy – Luke 1:41. This incident describes the impartation of Power from Jesus to John the Baptist.

John the Baptist never baptized Jesus physically. This can be evidenced from the Scriptures – Matthew 11:2–6; Luke 7:18 – 23. When John the Baptist was arrested and remanded in prison, he sent his disciples to find out from Jesus whether he was the expected Messiah or would they wait for another! If John had known and met (in fact baptized) Jesus physically, these enquiries would not have been necessary.

The story also goes that Jesus was the last to be baptized (Luke 3:21). This verse attempts to explain that Jesus (including all Messiahs) was the last to come with all concluding powers. Every Messiah comes last after having sent prophets as forerunners.

In conclusion, John never met Jesus in person. He only saw Jesus in revelations, and therefore could not have physically baptized him. It is not possible; for John was just a prophet, and Jesus a Messiah. Indeed, it is anti-creation, and anti-nature for a prophet to baptize a Messiah. In a very crude comparison, it is a little similar to a Reverend Priest blessing his Holiness, the Pope. It doesn't happen. A son cannot bless his father etc – Hebrew 7:7

Verse 14 John resisted surrendering the Power back to Jesus. But Jesus prevailed on him and retrieved the power.

CHAPTER 4– THE TEMPTATION OF JESUS– THE BATTLE OF THE MIND AND SPIRIT

Verse 1, 2 Desert or Wilderness refers to Mind that has gone into thinking or pondering about spiritual matters; whereas Devil or Satan is the Mind that follows the dictates of the body/flesh.

No Messiah ever fasts physically. That a Messiah fasted forty (40) days and forty (40) nights means He did not "eat" spiritual "food" until He clocked four hundred thousand (400, 000) levels of consciousness i.e. until He realized Himself as Spirit. At the end of these 400,000 years, He became hungry for speaking and teaching the things of the Spirit.

For instance, Moses fasted forty (40) days and forty (40) nights at Mount Horeb:

> *"I was on the mountain at the time, receiving the contract which Jehovah had made with you – the stone tablets with the Laws inscribed upon them. I was*

> *there for forty days and forty nights, and all that time I ate nothing. I didn't even take a drink of water. At the end of those forty days and nights the Lord gave me the contract, the tablets on which he had written the commandments he had spoken from the fire-covered mountain while the people had watched below"*– Deut 9:9-11; Deut 9:18; Deut 10:10 (TLB).

Moses was simply saying that when he realized himself as Spirit after 400,000 years, awareness of the knowledge of the Supreme Spirit came upon him; and he began to teach the people the true message of the Spirit. Mountain means being in the spirit. Stone tablets represent a righteous Heart.

And so when Jesus realized himself as Spirit, a battle raged on between his Spirit, Mind and Body *"....to be tempted of the Devil." "Hunger"* here refers to urge or great desire to teach the true message of the Spirit.

Verse 3 Stone refers to Heart whereas bread means spiritual message that can accommodate all situations, whatsoever. In the revelation, the carnal mind advised Jesus that having realized Himself, he should soften his heart to accommodate insults and problems that will come his way. That he should develop a large heart to endure and absorb the imminent suffering and experiences. Indeed, that Jesus should be tolerant.

Therefore, "*…changing stones into loaves of bread*" means converting your (strong) heart into the spiritual message that can accommodate all kinds of situations. This advice (and not really a *temptation*) was to prepare Jesus for his mission. Jesus learnt patience and tolerance in view of what he was going to encounter.

Verse 4 Jesus concurred: obedience to every word of God is what we need.

Verse 5, 6 'Go and tell the people you are the Messiah, and they will clap and welcome you.' "*…They will prevent you from smashing on the rocks below*" means that people will welcome him.

Verse 7 Jesus silenced his Mind by reminding it that his time has not yet come.

Verse 8, 9 His carnal Mind again tells Jesus to quit his Mission and go into the world in order to acquire material wealth.

Verse 10 Jesus encouraged himself to continue with the Mission of the Spirit he has been called to.

• *Calling of Jesus' disciples*

Verse 12– 22 This was a revelation regarding the calling of his twelve (12) disciples. Peter and Andrew were not fishermen in real life. They were in reality men who love and desire to serve God (Truth Seekers). They are described as commercial fishermen because they are seeking God, visiting and attending to so many spiritual organizations in a bid to find God.

Verse 23–25 This is a conclusion of Jesus Mission – healed every kind of sicknesses and diseases. The rest of the story in these verses were rendered spiritually i.e. in revelations. In reality enormous crowds never followed him. Nevertheless, He had followers.

Chapters 5, 6, and 7 – **Jesus encourages his Apostles**

The Apostles and other disciples were worried over mundane matters. They were discouraged and dispirited in the course of their journey to eternal life (Salvation). Here Jesus speaks to them.

Chapter 5:3 *"Poor in Spirit"* are those who admit they do not know anything spiritually, but are seeking. They desire spiritual messages and teachings. *"….Humble men…"* (TLB)

CHAPTER 8

Verse 1 *"….came down the hillside"*: Jesus came down from his divine nature and had to blend the message to the level of their understanding.

Verse 2–17 The healing sessions were revelations. Real healing takes place, first in the spirit. Oftentimes, a person receives a revelation of release from a bondage; a saving from an attack or a healing of a disease. The time and space it takes to manifest physically may be unrelated to the revelation earlier seen.

Verse 23 *'Then he got into the boat'*: This is rendered in the spirit i.e. it is a revelation, as in verse 1 above. *Boat* refers to the body. Each time Jesus is teaching spiritual messages, he is out of his body (boat) i.e. he assumes his spiritual essence in order to deliver the message of the Spirit. Afterwards he goes back into his physical body (boat) in order to attend to other physical or mundane activities other than spiritual, e.g. eating, sleeping etc.

Verse 24 After the teachings, trouble, noise and mob actions started. *Waves and storms* refer to 'dust' or reactions raised or triggered off by his alleged heresy (teachings)

Verse 26 Jesus talked to the mob and calmed them down using his teachings.

Verse 28, 29 These men are crude, mundane, carnal and gross materialistic (*demon possessed*). These people are terrible; spiritually dead, arrogant and haughty, because of material wealth they have acquired.

Verse 30–32 They accosted Jesus, challenging his audacity in teaching people spiritual messages. But Jesus used them for a "*show*". They begged to be cast into other dirty minds (*pigs*). Indeed, Jesus collected those dirty minds (from the two men); cast them into other similar dirty minds and the troubles of this world consumed them through accidents, earthquakes, other calamities etc.

CHAPTER 9

Verse 15 At the exit of Jesus, the disciples could fast or do all such other things to find God. But as far as Jesus is still with them, they didn't need to fast as an aid to hearing from God; and understanding Him. This is because the Messiah is with them, in flesh and blood; they can comfortably find the answer to whatever issues that confront them.

Verse 16–17 **Parable of Old and New Names:**

Old garments and old wineskin refer to the previous Persons or Minds that had used the old Name and old (previous) teachings of the Messiah. These old name and old teachings have thus become false because of carnal interpretation by false teachers. Nevertheless, the old name had saved people in the past. But there is a new name that will save people NOW.

On the other hand *new cloth and new wineskin* are the new Minds that will accept the new name of the Messiah.

Therefore, in this context, old wine (name) refers to the name of Moses whereas the new wine is the new name of Jesus.

Verse 18–32 All the recorded healings and miracles took place in the revelations. At their physical manifestations, they were not compiled alongside for the purpose of comparison. However, they would have been verbally confirmed and celebrated.

Verse 35 Jesus never physically went into the Jewish Synagogues. But in the Spirit i.e. in the revelations, his mind was always in the Synagogues urging the Priests to listen and understand Him.

CHAPTER 10

Verse 5–6 The *Gentiles* are the church-goers; the *Samaritans* are good people like the charitable organizations, the NGO's etc, whereas the *people of Israel* refer to the priests and the ordained.

Verse 14–15 Any city or home that doesn't receive his teachings will be destroyed in the Judgment Days – the three days of darkness.

CHAPTER 11

Verse 2–3 ***Implication or Significance of the Question in Verse 3:***

John the Baptist never saw nor met Jesus physically. This rules out the possibility of John ever baptizing Jesus at River Jordan as recorded in the Scriptures. Their encounter was in the Spirit; when Jesus withdrew the power he had bestowed on him. Recall when Virgin Mary, the Mother of Jesus visited Elizabeth, the mother of John the Baptist. Elizabeth was six months pregnant. The Bible recorded that as Virgin Mary greeted, the babe in the womb of Elizabeth leapt for joy.

Verse 7–11 ***Twin Appearance***: Prophets come first and Messiah follows.

Verse 12 "*And from the days of John the Baptist until now the Kingdom of Heaven suffereth violence and the violent taketh it by force…*" KJV The violent here refers to the carnal pastors and prophets who think that spiritual matters are physical – flesh and blood.

Verse 14, 15 Jesus teaches the concepts of *Reincarnation.*

Verse 25, 26 Popes, prophets, pastors and priests have employed all kinds of strategies and 'occultism' to understand God, but have failed due to wrong foundation.

Verse 26– 31 Method of bridging the Mind and Spirit is lighter and simpler with Jesus. His teachings are simple and not as hard as in the churches and synagogues: strenuous, unnecessarily long, mal-nourishing, stressful prayers and unhealthy fasting; going to the mountains and rivers for bathe and ablution – the so-called 'spiritual cleansing.'

CHAPTER 12

Verse 1–8 The disciples were not physically hungry. Rather they were '*hungry*' to preach the good news of the coming of the Messiah. However, they were preaching on an authorized day of the week.

Corn signifies the multitude of people. It is reported that the disciples picked the ears or heads of corn. These are left-over corns. *Left-Over Corns* refer to the down-trodden masses – the truck pushers and ordinary people etc. But the Churches had picked the professionals – medical doctors, bankers, rich men and women. The latter are the *main corn.*

Verse 9–30 Again Jesus healed several sicknesses and did some miracles. As usual these occurred in the Spirit – they are revelations and visions.

Verse 31–32 Any trifling (heresy or blasphemy) with the Mind and Body of the Messiah can be ignored but any such misdemeanor against the NAME of the Messiah (the name of the Messiah is the name of the Supreme Spirit – the Holy Spirit) shall be a charge against the person in Judgment.

For instance, you can say, this man, or this fellow (referring to the Messiah) is crazy, stupid etc; but if you say "Dara Ndu or Jesus is stupid etc," you are culpable. You will continue to pay with your life for eternity, for 'Dara Ndu or Jesus' is the name of the Supreme Spirit – *The Holy Spirit.*

Verse 33 *Snakes* refer to physically-minded people, *the Egyptians* or carnal people.

Verse 43– 45 If after receiving the messages of the Spirit and you backslide, you will be worse than before.

CHAPTER 13– JESUS TEACHES IN PARABLES

Verse 11 Only the disciples are permitted to know the secrets of the understanding of the spiritual messages e.g. snake is mind; Adam refers to Spirit whereas Eve stands for flesh or body etc.

Why Jesus uses Parables – Mankind is doomed for destruction. They have not matured to the point of understanding or taking in spiritual teachings. Even if plain language is used to explain the things of the Spirit, they will still not understand, accept or believe them. See Isaiah 6: 9-10; Hebrew 5:11

Verse 24–30 The *good seeds* refer to the spiritual teachings; the *weeds* are false teachings; the *farmer* is the Messiah. The *farmer's men* are the prophets whereas the *harvesting time* is the Judgment day.

Verse 31–32 *Tiny mustard seed* refers to the small group comprising of the Messiah (Himself) and His Apostles. The *largest of plant* is the magnitude this small group has expanded into. *Birds* are the people all over the Universe.

Verse 33 The message will get to every nook and cranny of the world. Today, Christianity (founded on the message of Jesus Christ) has spread far and wide, globally.

Verse 44–46 Jesus was jeered at for selling off his properties and household items in the course of his Mission. He responded with these parables. *Treasure* is the true Message of the Spirit.

Verse 47–50 Jesus was accosted on the dangers of his followers leaving the mission. He responded with this parable.

Dara Ndu does not use parables. He speaks in plain language. The reason the Spirit is delaying in His Work is because mankind is not yet ready to receive the message. Time must be ripened, with the unfolding of World events, before the message explodes.

When a person realizes he is Spirit, he thus enters the Kingdom of God (Heaven).

CHAPTER 14

Verse 1–12 The story of the beheading of John the Baptist was a revelation of display of anger by Herodias which culminated in the sacrifice of the head of the prophet.

In real life situation, however, Herodias masterminded the killing of John the Baptist. She pressurized King Herod to kill him. John was killed by hanging. But his head was not physically carried in a tray.

Verse 14 '…*Jesus came out of the wilderness…*' TLB '*Jesus came out of the boat…*' GNV Both phrases are synonymous. Wilderness refers to thinking, pondering or meditating. Jesus reflects and meditates on the spiritual messages he delivers to his followers. It is similar to being on the mountain. So when Jesus comes out of the wilderness or comes down from the mountain, he is loaded and equipped with spiritual messages for the people.

In the same vein, when Jesus comes out of the boat, he is no longer in his physical body; he is no longer pre-occupied with the routine, mundane and physical personal pastimes. He is busy teaching spiritual messages. In fact, this was a revelation concerning the teaching sessions of Jesus Christ.

Verse 15 The disciples of Jesus were convinced that the crowd do not understand the kind of messages he taught. They therefore urged the crowd to go back to their churches where they can get their usual kind of teachings (food). It is late to help them, since they can no longer be saved.

Verse 16 –19 Jesus taught them the sciences of Creation. He first taught his disciples who in turn passed them on to the people.

Bread refers to spiritual messages. Two (2) fish represent Water and Fire (Female Spirit and Male Spirit). Five (5) loaves stand for five (5) elements of Creation: *Water, Fire, Earth, Air, and Sky (Ether).*

Verse 20 They listened to the teachings and were satisfied.

Verse 21 The 4,000 (*not 5,000)* men represent 400,000 levels of consciousness of human existence before the attainment of self-realization. What was seen in the revelations was the number of years or levels of consciousness the people have passed through; it was not really the population of people listening to Jesus' teaching.

Those that will receive this message are men (*Nwoku,* not *Nwami*) who have attained 350,000 to 400,000 levels of consciousness.

The fragments, leftovers or scraps referred to in verse 20 are the remaining issues that were not understood by the people. And the basis of the message is Trinity

(12= 1+2= 3): *Mmuo, Mmuo-Okike, Mmuo-Ozi* – the origin and foundation of the spiritual teachings.

Verse 22–27 This is a revelation concerning the *arrest, trial, death and resurrection of Jesus*. Problems had just started for the Apostles. *Winds and waves* refer to acrimony, reactions and dust raised by the teachings of Jesus Christ. *That the wind was blowing against him* suggests that detractors were tracking him, planning and plotting to kill him. Jesus was indeed in trouble.

Verse 28–30 Peter was following at a distance during Jesus' travails and troubles. But when the challenges became so much (*strong wind*), he denied Jesus (*started sinking into the water*)– Chapter 26:69 – 75; John 18:15 – 18

Verse 31 Recall when Peter denied Jesus, the latter looked back at the former – to remind him that He, Jesus is still the Messiah, all odds notwithstanding.

Verse 32-33 Afterwards, Jesus resurrected. And His Apostles worshipped him.

Verse 34–36 These are the poor in Spirit– needing spiritual assistance. They came to Jesus as *sick folks* in revelations, as seen by the Apostles, afflicted in one way or the other.

CHAPTER 15

Verse 2 The Jewish leaders and Pharisees are protesting that despite the fact that the disciples of Jesus do not follow the rules and regulations of Jewish priesthood, they were allowed by Jesus to preach and teach spiritual messages. Recall that the Apostles are not ordained priests, but ordinary men.

Verse 3 But Jesus cautioned them, putting it to them that they worship man-made traditions rather than spiritual laws.

Verse 11–20 '*Not that which goeth into the mouth defilteh a man; but that which cometh out of the mouth…*'KJV Self-righteousness, consisting of strict obedience to the church dogmas (man-made traditions) does not make someone righteous or holy. Rather it is what one thinks or says.

Verse 24 The *Jews* are the priests, the ordained. *Gentiles* are church-goers – members of the congregation. Messiahs always and usually come for the priests– Hosea Chapter 5. The priests deceive and mislead the people. And so the Messiah comes, first to expose the priests; and thereafter turns over to the people to help them. Besides, if the priests can understand the Messiah, they can pass on the messages to the congregation with ease. See Ezek.34; Jer.23; Matt.23.

Verse 25–31 Jesus persisted in order to test the woman's faith since he knew the woman would not understand his teachings. Nevertheless, the woman insisted and had her daughter healed. But these healing sessions were seen in visions. No Messiah carries out healing of physical ailments. He rather heals the mind through his spiritual messages.

Verse 34 *Seven loaves* refer to the bodies at Creation: six (6) bodies– Aquatics, Plants/Trees, Insects, Animals, Human beings – and the final stage (body) of Self-awareness or Self-realization at which one knows he is Spirit.

CHAPTER 16

Verse 3 '*…but you can't read the obvious signs of the time!*' – Jesus rebuked them because they could not recognize nor understand that the Messiah has come; and yet all the World events are pointing to the End of Age. He particularly mocked their inability to use their highly sophisticated meteorological equipment to interpret the signs in the sky – the imminent and inevitable Final Judgment. Disappointedly, he walked out on them– not succumbing to their mindless and unreasonable demand for miracles.

Verse 5 Afterwards the disciples forgot all the messages he had taught them.

Verse 18 '*You are Peter, a Stone; and upon this rock I will build my church; and all the power of hell shall not prevail against it*' – It is at this level of spiritual maturity and awareness ("*Jesus is the Messiah, Christ, the Son of the Living God*") that His (Jesus') Mission will be founded and established. In other words, it is on that kind of Righteous Heart (*Stone or Rock*) that the Mission of Jesus will be anchored and built.

Jesus' words in verse 18 did not bestow nor arrogate on Peter, the head of the early church; neither did they make him the first Pope as widely but erroneously believed by Roman Church. Jesus only used his confession to illustrate the kind of Heart that will receive His spiritual messages/teachings.

Verse 23 Jesus referred to the same Peter as *Satan*– because the latter began to think like a carnal man. A while ago, he was referred to as a *Righteous Heart*, but now, a *Satan.* This adds credence to the fact that Jesus was not institutionalizing Peter with those words in verse 18. Jesus was simply recommending his Confession.

Verse 24 Do not be materialistic and carnal. *Cross* refers to human physical problems.

Verse 25 If you suffer physically on account of Him, you will be restored; if you are killed, you will gain eternal life.

Verse 28 When they reincarnate, they will see Jesus on His Return.

CHAPTER 17

Verses 1–9 This is a vision. *'And as they came down from the mountain, Jesus charged them, saying, Tell the vision to no man, until the Son of man be risen again from the dead.'* Verse 9 KJV In this vision, Jesus transfigured into his past incarnations in the presence of His Apostles. Indeed it was Moses and Melchizedek that appeared; not Elijah – for Elijah was a Prophet, and so cannot be in the order or lineage of the Messiahs.

'….high mountain apart (the top of high and lonely hill)' (verse 1) also signifies they were in the Spirit.

Verses 11–13 John the Baptist was the reincarnate of Elijah. Matt.11:14, 15.

Verse 21 The Apostles have not absorbed the spiritual message because they are not yet hungry for spiritual food. *Umuazi Jesus eriwebeghi nri nke mmuo.*

Verse 27 this was a revelation. The *fish* refers to a wealthy member of the Mission. He helps Jesus and His Apostles anytime they are in financial need. And so when they were confronted by the Tax Authority, Jesus sent Peter to this secret member who bailed them out by providing money for the payment of the taxes.

CHAPTER 18

Verses 21–22 One cannot forgive unless he knows the truth: truth about Creation and its corresponding Laws. The offended must recognize the offender in him and vice versa. It does not matter if the offender repents or not.

Jesus used *'Seventy times seven'* to encourage his Apostles to ultimately forgive their offenders.

CHAPTER 19

Verses 1–12 Jesus advises on divorce and marriage. It was not a teaching or Law. Neither is it a Command. It is a suggestion applicable to whoever may accept it.

Now listen to the teachings of Dara Ndu in these regards: If God does not join a couple i.e., if a marriage is not spiritual, it cannot withstand the test of time. It is therefore, advisable to dissolve such marriage in order to save the lives and dignity of the partners.

It is absolutely lawful for one to marry. It is a law in Creation; for that is the only way to be complete as a human being. Remember that an individual person is split specie. Therefore, coming together in a union with an opposite sex completes the individual.

However, due to a past karma, one may be compelled not to marry in a particular earth life. This does not mean he had not married previously. No one had existed as a conscious spirit without marriage, at one point or the other.

Warning! If a person does not marry, he will not make the kingdom of Heaven because he would still have remained split specie. He cannot realize God thereby.

Divorce is advisable when both partners were not previously joined spiritually. For example, a marriage contracted purely on gross materialistic basis will eventually crack. At such a time, it is spiritually imperative to dissolve it and let the individuals go their separate ways. Otherwise, the consequences will be terrible for both.

Verses 16–24 Jesus advised the Rich Young Ruler to help the poor and detach himself from his wealth. Only then, could he begin to understand his teachings.

Verses 25–26 It is only by the Power of the Holy Spirit that one can be saved. It is by commission and appointment of the Spirit, considering one's cycle of consciousness so far, that one can earn or attain eternal life– Chapter 16: 16–19. Apostle Paul once confessed it was by the Power of the Holy Spirit that he knew that Jesus was the Messiah.

Indeed, as soon as a person clocks 400,000 years of consciousness, he gains Salvation. Nevertheless, in the course of this journey (towards this mark) – say from 350,000 years – he could be permitted to cross the path of a Messiah. And as he continues to listen and experience His teachings, he attains Salvation or Eternal Life.

CHAPTER 20

Verses 1–16 This is an illustration of what was happening in His (Jesus') Mission. Every person who joins the mission, irrespective of date, receives the same eternal life. But the disciples wanted a bargain. They were interested in what they would gain exceptionally, from following Jesus. Hence they protested when they realized that other members who joined much later would receive the same reward. See Chapter 19: 27-28; 20: 20-28.

Verses 29–34 This was a revelation. Jesus opened their eyes through His Spiritual teachings. As a result, they joined his mission as members.

CHAPTER 21

Verses 1–11 This is a revelation of the Triumphant Entry of Jesus. *Donkey* refers to young and unblemished spiritual power. *Palm fronts* (branches of Palm trees) signify victory – the Spirit has conquered the Mind. They also represent those that have acknowledged his teachings or minds that follow the Spirit. Those that spread their garments along the road are those that will help Jesus in his mission.

Verses 12–16 This is also a revelation. In reality, Jesus was speaking against the false messages (of prosperity, etc.) prevalent in the temples and Synagogues. It would tantamount to civil offence for Jesus to enter their temple; and begin to physically drive people away; and destroy their properties. He did not have such physical audacity.

Verses 18–20 This is yet another revelation. Jesus defeated a '***very big carnal man of God***' with a mammoth crowd in a debate. His large crowd dispersed because they discovered there were no spiritual fruits in him. He had only crowd and money.

The *fig tree* refers to the pastor, the big man of God; the *leaves* symbolize the mammoth crowd; and the *figs* are spiritual fruits.

When the congregation discovered their pastor had nothing to offer after all, they deserted his church – *the fig tree withered*!

CHAPTER 22

Verses 1–14 Jesus explains the efforts made by the Messiahs in calling people to come forward and receive spiritual messages. The Messiah would first send his prophets; but mankind will not receive them. The prophets would be mistreated. Thereafter, He would send Apostles to win over ordinary, simple and lay people.

These efforts notwithstanding, there could still be others who would not accept the teachings nor align with others (*not wearing wedding robes provided them*). These are the categories of people that will be consumed at the Final Judgment.

Many indeed are invited, but few are chosen.

Verse 29–32 Jesus was referring to spiritual resurrection. It is only the physical body that suffers physical death. Physical marriage between a man and a woman has no connection with resurrection. But when spiritual marriage occurs between the Mind and the Spirit, resurrection takes effect. The individual is thereby said to have realized himself as Spirit.

CHAPTER 23

Jesus rebukes and reviles the false teachers and prophets in a very plain language.

CHAPTER 24

Verses 29–31 Take special note that verses 30 and 31 should precede verse 29.

Verses 30 '*The Signal of my coming*' refer to the Rainbow Cross (Genesis 9:8-17). This '*coming*' does not refer to the Advent of the Messiah but the explosion of the anger of the Lord– Amos 5: 18-20.

'*Angels with the sound of a Trumpet blast*' refers to volcanic eruptions, earthquakes, typhoon, poverty, terrible diseases etc. These are persecutions.

Verses 29 After these persecutions, the three days of darkness will commence. See Revelation Chapter 9.

CHAPTER 25

Verses 14–46 Those that put in practice the spiritual messages of the Messiah will be given more responsibilities with its accompanying rewards. But those that did not would be consumed at the Final Judgment.

CHAPTER 26

Verses 26–29 *Bread* in this context refers to the *body* of Jesus which symbolizes Water. *Wine* stands for the *blood* of Jesus which represents Fire. To eat of the body of Jesus and drink of his blood means to accept *Water and Fire as Spirit*. This is the pre-requisite for Eternal Life.

Last Supper or Passover Feast refers to the last message and physical contact from Jesus before He goes back to unite with the Supreme Spirit.

Verse 51, 52 Peter could be charged for a criminal offence, if in reality, he had cut off Malchus' ear, just because he was in the company of those who came to arrest Jesus.

The High Priest in his authority and office had found Jesus guilty; passed a death sentence on Him; and dispatched soldiers to arrest Him. Now watch this! Don't you think that Peter, cutting off his servant's ear tantamount to adding insult to injury?

But let's assume it happened physically. Is it possible that Jesus could just pick up the cut-off ear and put it back instantly without surgical operations?– Luke 22:51. If it did happen physically, it will have been anti-nature. It would negate the adamantine Laws of Creation which Jesus, the Messiah had come to fulfill. This incident was a mere vision.

Now listen to the interpretation: The sword refers to the Truth. Peter told Malchus the truth about the Messiah-ship of Jesus Christ. Malchus, unfortunately, has never heard of the message of Christ. This truth as related by Peter tingled his ear and made him very uncomfortable and embarrassed.

Jesus, noticing this persuaded Malchus to ignore and discountenance what Peter had told him. Jesus then gave him the usual teaching he was accustomed to; in fact what he (Malchus) wanted and had always heard in the Temples and Synagogues.

Therefore, cutting off Malchus' ear refers to sudden taking in of unprecedented but unwanted message. In the spirit or revelation, his ear will fall off the ground. *"Returning"* or *"putting back"* of the ear means telling him the usual teachings he has always been accustomed with– Luke 22:51.

CHAPTER 27

Verses 3–10 Judas Iscariot repented:

a. He confessed he never knew Jesus would be arrested. He was a businessman who wanted to con the High Priests and collect their money. Judas was also a member of a rebel group involving Barabbas, the criminal. Their mission was to cause strife and insurrection against the Roman Government with a bid to chasing them out of the Jewish Land.

So Judas Iscariot thought he would hoodwink the high priest with a sure belief that Jesus would do magic and disappear.

b. Judas did not spend the thirty (30) pieces of silver. He returned it (restitution).

c. He hanged himself (committed suicide), thereby removing the body that betrayed his Lord and Master.

d. Besides, Judas fulfilled his part of Jesus' Mission as prophesied in *Isaiah 53*.

e. Against this backdrop, Judas Iscariot made it in the Kingdom of Heaven.

CHAPTER 28

Verses 1–20 When a Messiah discards his physical body, the revelation of his resurrection comes to his Apostles three days after. This is the Proof of His true Messiahship. Any Messiah who does not resurrect is not a true one. For avoidance of doubt, the physical body of the messiah does not resurrect. The resurrection is of His Mind/Soul and its merger with the Spirit.

OTHER PROOFS OF A TRUE MESSIAH ARE:

- The First Miracle– he explains the sciences of Creation
- His teachings will be unparalleled
- His Name will save whoever calls it.

LUKE

CHAPTER 8: 1 – 3 AND CHAPTER 10: 38 – 41 – JESUS PHYSICAL PRIVATE PASTIMES

Marriage: Every true Messiah that has walked the surface of this earth had always come with consorts. These are women who surrender their lives to Him. Examples are Noah, Lot and Moses, even Lord Krishna and Lord Rama. They all had families.

Indeed, Martha was Jesus' first consort. Unfortunately, the Bible was very silent about His pastimes with Mary Magdalene. Recall the quarrel that ensued between Martha and Mary Magdalene as recorded in *Chapter 10: 38– 41*. Many other women joined Jesus after he declared His Mission. Mary Magdalene also gave her life at that time and started living with Jesus as His consort. When Martha left in annoyance and out of jealousy for Mary Magdalene, the latter took over the running of the Royal Family. And she had a child for Jesus.

Does this sound ridiculous and incredible? Listen! Jesus' paternity does not in any way extenuate His Supreme essence. It is all about His physical personal pastime. Any person who does not accept that Jesus had consorts is anti-Christ, anti-God and anti-Creation. See! Whether Jesus had consorts or not, is not the real reason of His Mission. You must hold his spiritual teachings with great tenacity.

Listen! The problem with the Christians is that they are apathetic; they do not make effort to really experience God. They only swallow hook, line and sinker any trash they are told about God – mere belief; no conviction. They have carnally established conditionality and criteria for assessing and measuring who and what God should look like. Very unfortunate!

But hear this: every true messiah that will walk and work on the surface of this earth can never administer His Mission without his consorts. Messiahs do not marry wives in the world's conventional manner. They work with consorts. Nevertheless they can be referred to as 'wives' in today's parlance. As far as the messiah is concerned, consorts are house-devotees (*Chapter 8:1-3*). They take care of his personal physical needs, including raising of children, if need be.

These pastime activities do not make Him less a messiah. The Bible compilers were deliberately silent about these things because they do not have anything to do with the Salvation He brought.

Besides, Messiahs come specifically and firstly for the salvation of women and children. He comes to change their lives from material illusions to spiritual awareness; and bring morality in their homes. And so how could a messiah avoid women?

Moses was seriously acquainted with Pharaoh's daughter. Miriam was his first 'wife'. Moses got 'married' to Zipporah, Jethro's daughter (*Exodus 2: 21-22*). And later, he married a Cushite woman, resulting to criticism from Miriam and Aaron (*Numbers 12:1-3*).

The Bible recorded that Moses perfected in all "*Egyptian Arts*" (*Acts 7:22*)– meaning that he did everything any other human being could do in the physical body. These pastimes or 'drama' did not taint his divinity; neither did they reduce his authority as the deliverer of the people of Israel.

His physical nature worked according to the physical laws of creation whereas his spiritual nature obeyed the spiritual laws of the Supreme Spirit. The messiah cannot carry the body of an animal or that of a tree. He must come with a human body (*I John 4:1-3*). There is no conflict between his physical and spiritual essences.

CHAPTERS 23 AND 24– JESUS' DEATH AND RESURRECTION

Chapter 23: 44-56 At the end of His mission here on earth, more than 2,000 years ago, Jesus discarded his physical body through a process generally referred to as physical death or clinically certified death (CCD). No messiah ever dies. He goes back to His original nature– the Supreme Spirit.

Chapter 24:1-49 After three days of physical death, his mind/soul resurrects to merge with the Supreme Spirit. This is the proof of every true messiah.

No true messiah ever resurrects with his physical body. Neither does resurrection ever takes place physically. It shall tantamount to anti-Christ, anti-God and anti-Creation. Resurrection is therefore a purely spiritual experience.

Is it not surprising then, that the synoptic gospels' accounts of the resurrection of Jesus were quite differently told– *Matthew 28:1-20; Mark 16:1-20; Luke 24:1-53; John 20:1-29*? Did Jesus resurrect four times? No! Each reporter was relating the visions of Jesus' resurrection according to how he or she received it (*Luke 24: 22-24 GNV*). So you can see that the event was not a physical manifestation. Otherwise the stories would have been identical.

Moses also resurrected. The Bible recorded that his body was not found where he was buried– *Deut 34:6*. This is in line with Jesus' story– *that his body was not found in the grave.* The body referred to here, is not a physical body, but mind/soul body.

Therefore, it is a blatant lie, a falsehood and in fact a deception for anybody to insinuate that Jesus did not physically die on the cross; and that his disciples stole his physical body and took him to India where he lived for 120 years!

Verse 50–52 This is part of the revelation concerning Jesus' resurrection. It is only the physical body the Messiah will use on His Return that will see the Spirit descending onto the earth. No other person can see it. (Recall, the messiah and the Supreme Spirit had become one – 'I and my Father are one').

That spiritual experience (the messiah/Supreme Spirit descending on the new body at return) is the basis of assurance and confidence in His present Mission. And so despite the inevitable, but harrowing physical challenges he experiences, he remains steadfast and humble – *Luke 17:25.*

JOHN

CHAPTER 1

Verse 1, 2 Before the physical creation, the Word already existed, and the Word was with the Spirit. That Word was OM, and the Word was the same with The Spirit.

The pronoun, 'He' or 'Him' should be replaced with 'it'. 'He' and 'Him' personalized the Spirit and gave it a form. But the Spirit does not have a form. Nevertheless, the compilers of the Bible had Jesus in mind at the point of reporting.

Verse 3 Through the Word, the Spirit made all things. Not one thing in all creation was made without the Word, OM.

Verse 4 OM was the source of Life, and this Life brought Light to mankind.

Verse 5 The Light shines in the darkness and the darkness has never put it out. At OM vibration, there was Light. That Light has continued to be since physical creation. The darkness has not put it out – there shall never be a going-back to primordial age (the age before creation).

Verses 6-10 That Light is the Supreme Spirit– "*ihee ahu*". Everything is inside it – all things created. The Spirit is living in the hearts of all living things. It is in the body of human beings that the Spirit is realized. All other bodies want to evolve to (become) human body.

Verse 11-13 "*Born Again*" or"*Reborn*" refers to spiritual anointing; self-realization; self-awareness and consciousness; knowing oneself; having ripened spiritually; clocking 400,000 levels or years of human consciousness. It does not come by personal affirmation or declaration or by physical ceremonies of Church tradition. Neither does it happen through self-examination of personal idiosyncrasies and behavioral tendencies.

Verse 14 this verse should have preceded the introduction of the pronouns, 'He' or 'Him' as recorded in verses 2, 3 etc.

At the end of every 2,000 years, when mankind begins to deviate from the spiritual, The Supreme Spirit takes on a form (the word made flesh) in order to teach mankind. This 'form' is referred to as The Messiah, the Christ, the Avatar, the Savior.

Verse 19-23 No prophet knows himself. It is only the Messiah that tells who they are.

Verse 29-34 Dove means the Power of the Spirit. Baptism also refers to Power.

CHAPTER 2

Verses 1-11 ***The Story of Creation:*** The six (6) jars of water represent the six bodies of aquatic, plant/ trees, insects, birds, animals and man. The master of ceremony is the mind, in whose custody the created body of man was entrusted. The best wine that was served later refers to the last but the apex and most significant part of creation – Man, the beauty of Life.

The presence of the Holy Mother, Mary and Jesus represents Water and Fire respectively. Recall that it was Mother Mary who urged Jesus to provide more wine at the marriage feast.

Verses 14-16 *Whip* symbolizes making a mockery of them through His message of truth; it represents painful truth.

CHAPTER 3

Verse 5 Unless one '***knows***' that *Water* and *Fire* is Spirit, he cannot realize himself as Spirit i.e. he cannot enter the Kingdom of God. "***Know***" means experience; awareness; spiritual revelation confirming the fact of Water and Fire as The Spirit.

Verses 22-36 This incident occurred in revelation. To *baptize* here means to impart power, anointing and knowledge.

CHAPTER 4

Verses 16-19 The five (5) previous '*husbands*' refer to the first five bodies/specie created– aquatics, plant/ trees, insects, birds and animals. The sixth '*husband*' refers to the human body (specie) the Samaritan woman has now assumed.

In verse 17, the Samaritan woman answered she had no husband…. *"I am not married".* According to Jesus, the woman was truthful; because there is yet another "body" the woman must assume or take on before she earns Salvation (eternal Life). This seventh body shall come about at the woman's realization (awareness) that she is not this physical body or mind, but Spirit. Then the mind and Spirit shall have become one *(married together).* Put differently, having a husband or getting married is comparable to achieving eternal life i.e. the mind and Spirit uniting and becoming One (The Universal Spirit).

Verse 24 God is the The Supreme Spirit. *To worship Him in Spirit* means to have a personal communion or fellowship or communication or contact or relationship with Him through revelations and visions for directions.

To *worship Him in Truth* means internalizing the Laws of Creation; the Spiritual Laws – *I mara ihe mere eme* i.e. knowing the Truth; acquiring knowledge of creation in order to avoid delusion and deception.

REVELATION

CHAPTER 1

Verse 7 ***Jesus' Second Coming***: At His second coming, during which Judgment shall take place, everybody will see Him. Indeed, all will have reincarnated on earth to face judgment.

Coming with the clouds refers to this judgment: thunders, waves, earthquakes, hurricane etc. When these great world events begin to unfold, all eyes shall observe and witness them; including those who pierced Him. This is really, God in action. All nations will weep in sorrow and terror. This may appear to be the visible sign of His physical coming. But on the contrary, this is just the anger of God being unleashed upon mankind.

Jesus had declared in Matthew 24:30, "*They shall see the Son of Man coming in the clouds of heaven*". Now listen to Dara Ndu as He explains its meaning:

> *"When I spoke in the body of Jesus, I came upon the clouds. By this I did not mean the blue firmament but heaven or the kingdom of The Supreme Spirit; and from this heaven I descended upon the clouds. It means that I came with a physical body. <u>My physical body is the cloud that hides my Divinity from the people.</u>"*

> *As "clouds" are obstacles to the shining of the sun, so also, the clouds of doubts in the mind of worldly humanity hid the radiance of My Divinity as the Christ from the eyes of men. My body as Jesus was born of Mary, but My Spirit was of Oke Mmuo – The Supreme Spirit. The capacities of My human body were limited but the Power and Glory of My Spirit was vast, infinite and immeasurable.*

The word 'cloud' is figurative, depicting the concealing (beclouding) of the reality. Jesus' coming with the clouds therefore refers to this anger of God. But this Anger of the Lord and the physical coming of the Messiah always occur simultaneously. When the Messiah finally anchors in flesh and blood, the END has automatically set in.

Consider this: why would the whole nation wail and weep as He comes – an event that is supposed to usher in joy? That is simply judgment! Everybody will experience this tribulation. They will look up the sky, but will not see any '*figure*' except thunders, poisonous air, earthquakes, volcanoes and terrible things that will be happening in those days, Amos 5:18-23.

Rather than waiting for the day of the anger of the Lord, mankind should ask for and yearn for the day of the physical coming of the Messiah.

Verse 12-18 This description represent a form no one can see physically. They are mere allegories. For example, two sharp edged swords refer to two powerful Truths: *Mmiri na Oku* – Truths that are pointblank and uncompromised, *verse 16*. This is the foundation of all Truths. Verses 13-15 describe the spiritual form of the Messiah John could behold and understand. It does not represent the real image of the Spirit. For the Spirit does not have a form.

CHAPTER 2– MESSAGES TO THE CHURCHES

Verse 1-5 *the Church at Ephesus*: Physical problems among the members made their faith in the Lord to wane. When people start backsliding because unbelievers are taunting and making mockery of them, their unconditional love for God begins to diminish.

The candle stick (verse 5) is the power; the message imparted on them. If God switches off the light in a person, he withdraws (backslides) and the power (knowledge) in him becomes extinguished. If a person ceases to love the Messiah again, he will start picking holes in whatever He does. This is because the message and love go together.

But the truth is that if you love somebody, you see yourself inside him. That is what love signifies– seeing yourself through the eyes of that other person – *I fu na anya; ka I fu Chukwu n'anya onye ozo.* When you look into his black eyes and you are able to see him, then that person is something else – he is your enemy. You can kill him. But if you see yourself (which is certain), then be rest assured that you are inside of him. In other words, both of you are the same Spirit– but are wearing different cloaks called physical bodies.

Verse 6 *The licentious Nicolaitans* refer to false teachers; a race that do not know God; cities that reject the true teachings of the Spirit

Verse 7 The *fruit* referred to here is the message; the knowledge of the Spirit. Those who endure to the end will have this victory. These are people who have conquered and defeated the influences around them– family, parents, peers, colleagues etc. You must conquer these influences and remain steadfast to the teachings of the Messiah. Only then will God give you the fruits from the Tree of Life.

What are these *fruits and the Tree of Life*? Refer back to Genesis Chapter Two. The Tree of Life is the Supreme Spirit; the fruit is the knowledge of the Spirit. If you conquer the battles of this life (influences mentioned above), you become victorious.

But what are these battles? These are wars that rage every moment in our minds. The battle is not physical or carnal but spiritual. If it is possible to read people's mind, you will see a 'friend' physically smiling at you but releasing 'missiles and bombshell' at you. You could be dining with a 'friend' who is inwardly planning to harm you. That is why Apostle Paul told the *Ephesians* in *Chapter 6 verses 10 to 17* that the battle is not against flesh and blood, but against principalities and powers in the minds of people. These are the influences we have to defeat.

All those people who you declare as enemy are not your real enemies. Your real enemy is ignorance of the Laws of the Spirit– not a physical human being.

Verse 9–11 *the Church at Smyrna:* There are two types of death. The first is the physical death, and the second is the Mind death. The worst and painful thing that can happen to a man is to experience both. Of course the Spirit cannot die. But to die mentally is a colossal holocaust. Death is *only* for the physical body.

And so here, Jesus is talking about the death of the soul. It is a well-known fact that corruption is rife the world-over. Justice has long been killed. There is preponderance of sin and evil. The conscience of man has seared. (By the way, conscience comes from the mind; and it is only the mind that the Messiah comes to salvage.)

On the contrary, those who are saved i.e. those whose minds have been salvaged are exempted from this dreadful second death. Therefore, to die a second death means that the soul/mind is not salvaged. Jesus once said in *Matthew 16:26*, "*For what is a man profited, if he shall gain the whole world, and lose his own soul? Or what shall a man give in exchange for his soul*" KJV. Losing one's soul therefore, is the second death.

Again, everything a man does comes from the mind. And so if the creations therefrom are not in accordance with the Laws of the Spirit, that person's soul is dead. Put in another way, when a man is carnal and do not know God, his soul is dead. This is *second death– Hosea 4:6.*

But can somebody wear a physical cloak and experience second death? No! You cannot experience second death when you are in the flesh. Second death presupposes you will have experienced the first death, i.e. you will have dropped the physical body. And in the proceedings of the Judgment, *second death* automatically sets in, if found guilty.

Also when it is said of a physically living person, that he does not have conscience or that his conscience is dead, it is a sign that he will meet second death.

Verse 12–17 *the Church at Pergamos*: Before a man receives Salvation, he must conquer his mind; he must conquer the physical world. Only then would he have detached from materialistic influences and rested all worries.

Hidden Manna or secret nourishment refers to the teachings of the Messiah. White Stone represents pure heart or righteous heart. The New Name refers to the new name of Jesus, the Messiah, which is Dara Ndu. Only those who receive it know what it means. Dara Ndu is the name of the Supreme Spirit who incarnated in the physical body to salvage mankind, verse 17.

Verse 18–29 *the Church at Thyatira*: 'Jezebel' connotes wickedness at high places. Any woman who is cruel, insensitive and inconsiderate to the feelings of others can be addressed as such. Do you remember the story of Queen Jezebel, the wife of King Ahab, in Second Kings?

R*od* means straight or strictness. People will be compelled to keep according to the rules or Laws of God – *ruling them with iron rod,* verse 27. Those who overcome will be shining like stars because of the knowledge they show forth. These overcomers or conquerors are those who detached themselves from the physical world (Mind), verse 28.

CHAPTER 3– MESSAGES TO THE CHURCHES CONTINUED

Verse 1 *the Church at Sardis: "…he that has the Seven Spirits of God and the Seven Stars."* The Seven Spirits and Stars are the six (6) levels of the created bodies, plus the Self-Consciousness, namely:

1. Aquatics
2. Plants/Trees

3. Insects
4. Birds
5. Animals
6. Human Beings
7. The Self-Consciousness (as Spirit)

Verse 2, 3 If a person does not worship God in truth and spirit, all his deeds (tithes, church projects, evangelism etc.) are dead.

Verse 7 *the Church at Philadelphia:* David (not the biblical David you read about in the book of Samuel) means Beloved. Only the Lord is called Beloved. David also represents Conqueror. Therefore, who can best be described as The Beloved and Conqueror, if not the Supreme Spirit? Recall that the biblical David conquered Goliath? Again, in spiritual parlance, Goliath represents the Mind. We can then conclude by saying, in that context, that The Spirit conquered the Mind.

K*ey of David* means Knowledge of the Spirit. When you have this knowledge (key), you can open all doors– of illusion, delusion, confusion and darkness.

Verse 14–22 *the Church at Laodicea:" pure Gold…gold purified by fire…".* Pure Gold refers to message of the Truth; and Fire is the Knowledge.

CHAPTER 4– WORSHIP IN HEAVEN

Verse 2–3 '*The Throne*' is represented by the physical one at Dara Ndu's temple, including the surrounding flags.

The '*Twenty-four (24) Elders*' refer to the 6 (2+4) levels of created bodies, namely, the aquatics, plants/trees, insects, birds, animals and human beings.

When the Messiah comes, He is accompanied by the entire Universe. The elders in all the created bodies and He (Himself) make up the 7 (seven) Spirits. The elders in these levels of consciousness are the heads, having attained perfection. These elders are representing these bodies as 'Messiahs'. The Messiah in the human body represents the Supreme Spirit.

These elders would surround the Messiah physically around the Throne – but may not be seen by ordinary eyes.

Verse 4 These elders have attained Salvation. '*Clothed in white, with golden crowns upon their heads*' means they have attained Righteousness and Perfection.

Verse 5 His (the Messiah's) words are '*thunders and lightning*.'

Verse 6 His words are Truthful; no falsehood ('*shiny crystal sea*')

Verse 6–8 '*The Four Living Beings*' are the Powers of the Messiah. His powers come in different symbols, figures and objects, manifestations, depending on the spiritual position or standing of the visionary.

Verse 9–11 All living things worship the Supreme Spirit.

CHAPTER 5– MESSIAH (THE CHRIST) EXPLAINS THE SCIENCES OF CREATION

Verses 1-2 '*To break the Seal*': Today Dara Ndu is breaking the Seals: He is explaining the coded writings of the revelations of the Spirit; He is teaching the True Messages of the Spirit.

No body, in heaven, on earth, and beneath the earth can break the Seal except Dara Ndu.

The '*Seven Seals*' are: the Aquatics lives, plant/trees, insects, birds, animals, Man, and the Spirit (man at realization of self). These seals constitute the Spiritual Laws; they are the Seven Spirits also known as the Stars.

Dara Ndu clearly explains the bodies created; species of created bodies; years that the Spirit lives in the bodies; and stars that stand for, and give light to these created bodies. See Dara Ndu's commentaries on Genesis Chapter 1:6-31.

Verse 2 Who can decode the sciences of creation and explain the Spiritual Laws? Verses 2 to 7 refer to when Dara Ndu declared His Mission and explained to people what has taken place in the Spirit: that the Supreme Spirit has taken on a human form in order to explain its creations.

Verse 6-8 Only the Messiah can break open the Seal– the Lamb that was hitherto killed and now is alive. It was the same Jesus that was crucified.

If Jesus had appeared to John with a different body in the revelation, the latter would not have recognized Him. That is why John had continued to use the term, *'Lion of the Tribe of Judah'*. Jesus revealed Himself to John in His previous body. It is that *'Lion of Judah'* that continues to come. In fact it is that same *'Lion of Judah'* that has just come, but mankind has been blinded by gross materialism, illusion and carnality.

Jesus was described as Lamb because of His humility. However, He has come this time as Lion and Horse in the name and body of Dara Ndu.

Verse 9-14 The entire universe (all living things) are giving glory to the Messiah – the one that sits on the throne. In the spirit, it will be so magnificent, but only an infinitesimal manifestation will be at display here in the physical planet earth.

All are praising Him because He has conquered i.e. He has announced His Advent.

The *'New Song'* signifies saying and doing things differently from the old ways, (cf new wine and new garment: Matthew 9:16-17).

CHAPTER 6- PICTURE OF THE END TIMES

Verse 1-2 *'White Horse'* is the Truthful or Righteous Power. The *'bow'* is the Rainbow – the symbol of Power and Authority. Every revelation here is all about Him— the Messiah. He is the beginning. He is the cause of all happenings (world events). He is ready and prepared to go out, and conquer the world.

Verse 3 Today's world events have long been predicted. They have been programmed in the events and lives of men. Indeed the words of the revelations must be fulfilled and cannot lie, namely–

Verse 4 wars, battles and killings

Verse 5-6 hardship and deprivation; severe austere living; economic failures and financial crisis; global poverty, etc. Mankind is to be kept alive, but will suffer terribly on this earth.

Verse 7 famine and diseases

Verse 9 *'altar'* refers to the 'heart' of those who served the Lord.

Verse 12-17 the Final Onslaught – the three days and nights of darkness (the Final Judgment).

All these sufferings ought to make people come back to Him. Nevertheless, they would insist in practicing their religious dogmas to the highest height; but it will not save them. At the eleventh hour, they will prefer to die at the mountains. Having rejected Dara Ndu, they have spoiled their chances and opportunities for Salvation. Indeed, everybody will be rewarded according to his deeds.

CHAPTER 7– THE NINE (9) APOSTLES OF DARA NDU

Introduction: According to the sciences of numbers, numerical counting is limited to the following: 1, 2, 3, 4, 5, 6, 7, 8, 9, and 0. All other numerals are mere repetition or additions. For example, 11 (eleven) is obtained by adding numeral 1 (one) into eleven places.

And so the 144,000 must be reduced to a single digit such as 1 + 4 + 4 + 0 + 0 + 0 = 9. Therefore, the '*144,000 Children of Israel' (Jews)* are the 9 (nine) Apostles of Dara Ndu. These are the servants that are being awaited before the Great Tribulation (destruction) commences.

These nine (9) apostles are very dear to Him. It was for the sake of the twelve (12) apostles that Jesus died. These are people who understand His teachings. They would first take the messages, and thereafter disseminate them to mankind, *Matthew 14:19*. Each of the nine (9) apostles is mandated to convert sixteen thousand (16,000) persons, culminating to 144,000 persons. This process of conversion is very similar to modern Multi-Level Marketing System (MLM).

Dara Ndu cannot do without these chosen ones. But first they must be carefully identified and given the seal – the seal of the entire creation. This seal of God is the Covenant of God, the unfolding of the Knowledge of God. What is derailing the Final Judgment is that the selection of the nine (9) apostles has not been completed. That also explains why the Mission has not commenced in earnest. As soon as selection is completed, He will step aside. Recall when Moses was asked to hold his hand up: signifying the completion of His Messianic mandate. God then proceeded with its Judgment on the people of Israel.

Verse 3 '…*Placing the seal of God upon the foreheads…*' It is the Messiah that places His seal upon the foreheads of His servants.

Dara Ndu came with this seal– the mark of the Supreme Spirit. Once upon a time, there was a great contest in the spirit as to which seal among numerous 'seals' would ascend the Throne. Dara Ndu's Seal suddenly appeared at the centre of the Throne. And all other 'seals' and deities fell by the way sides.

Therefore, Dara Ndu's message (Seal), and Mission is the Reality. It is the Truth. As soon as a person crosses his path with Him (*very important!*), and He lays His hands on the person's forehead, the seal would have entered. Dara Ndu can also give him the physical seal– which carries His mark (Niike na Ebube).

Verse 4-8 Those nine (9) apostles will come from various tribes – Yoruba, Ibo, Ibibio, Efik, Hausa, Europeans, Americans, and Asians etc.

Verse 9 These 144,000 people, seen in revelations, are vastly enormous– a mammoth crowd. '*They were clothed in white with palm branches in their hand*', signifies that they have become righteous; have conquered their mind; and are victorious. This explains why, in Igbo tradition, palm branches are inserted in the grave of a dead person: the individual has escaped the bondage of the physical body. He is now free from attachment to the body and materialism. He has become a new creature wearing a new and different cloak. If he reincarnates, he will not come in that old body. He will wear a new one.

Verse 11-12 The twenty-four (24) Elders and four (4) Beasts/Living Beings are figures seen in the Spirit, but they represent similar phenomenon. If you are seeing in the Spirit, you will discover that there are twenty-four (24) Elders sitting around Dara Ndu on His Throne. These Elders, in accordance with the sciences of numbers are the six (6) (2+4) levels of Creation: Aquatic lives, Plants/Trees, Insects, Birds, Animals and Human Beings. Each of these levels of Creation has an Elder.

In the same way, a messiah comes in a human form, so does He come in the form of each of these other levels of Creation. These messiahs are the elders. They are elders because they have graduated to evolve into another live/body.

For all the human beings in existence today, Dara Ndu is their elder; who stands in as the Savior. He is representing both human beings and the Spirit. This is what (every) messiah does at the turn of each 2,000 years. If He hears from mankind, He relates to the Spirit; if He receives from the Spirit, He communicates mankind. This explains why Dara Ndu (in fact every messiah), not only has a human form, but He is also the Supreme Spirit.

The task of salvaging the Universe is the collective responsibility of these six (6) elders, plus the Spirit, making up the *Seven-fold Spirit and Stars*. It is not only man that needs salvation. Every other living thing– aquatic lives to animals– is striving to evolve into a human form for onward transition to self-realization.

These creatures will make effort to cross the path of the Savior so as to experience this process of Involution and Evolution. And it is only the messiah in the human form that makes this possible. The process occurs once every 2,000 years.

Verse 13-17 This is the revelation of the Salvation of these servants of God (144,000).

Salvation is different from physical destiny. Your physical destiny is what the Spirit promised or agreed to use your physical body to enjoy, achieve or experience. It is already programmed in consideration of the outworking of your previous earth-lives. This destination must come to pass, for it has been ordained.

And so whether the outcome of this destination is deprivation, distress, disease or prosperity, it does not affect your Salvation – which is your spiritual destiny. Your Salvation or the Savior cannot obviate or set aside your karmic reactions. However, if you are really devoted to Him, offering worshipful service unto Him, you will not experience the full weight or gravity of the karmic reactions. Rather you will pass through such events symbolically, *Matthew 11:28-30. (*KJV)

So if you have crossed the path of the Messiah, do not grumble or slip away or become discouraged as you experience your physical destiny. Both are mutually exclusive.

Hence Salvation is a more serious matter. Apostle Paul admonished that one should work out his salvation with fear and trembling, *Philippians 2:12.* (KJV)

Verse 14 Those servants have cleansed and purified their mind, intelligence, senses and body (i.e. were made righteous) by the knowledge of the teachings of Jesus Christ. This is what makes them '*virgins*'. Their virginity is not a carnal matter and should not be viewed physically. It is all about purity of heart nurtured and nourished by unblemished and undiluted Truth/message.

CHAPTER 8– SIGNS OF END-TIMES

These are initial events that will culminate toward the three days and nights of darkness – earthquakes, tsunamis, volcanic eruptions, etc.

Trumpets refer to thunder – each bringing forth different types of suffering. The *angels* are the messengers of God who will unleash havoc on mankind at this end-time.

Verse 1 The Seventh Seal belongs to Dara Ndu. A violent contest ensued in the Spirit in which all other seals that attempted to ascend the throne were thrown out. For as soon as Dara Ndu's seal took possession of the Throne, there was silence and calmness all over the heaven.

When Dara Ndu finally declared the Reality physically on planet earth, all other seals (messages) went underground – for there cannot be two seals.

Verse 3-5 The incense is like a trigger in a gun or the knob of a detonation in a process of blowing up a bombshell: the Power of God being released in the form of terrible smoke, poisonous gases, thunders etc. All deadly things will be invoked upon mankind.

God's people would be protected including their properties and pets. But the evil people were destroyed by thunders, lightning and earthquakes.

Verse 6-11 Different shades of sufferings are released at different times during the end-time

Verse 12 All those sufferings culminated toward the three days and nights of complete darkness.

Verse 13 The three remaining angels will blow the trumpets during the three successive days and nights of darkness.

CHAPTER 9- THREE DAYS AND NIGHTS OF DARKNESS

Verse 1-2 Catastrophe, problems, poisonous gases, rumbles and unbearable situations will overtake the earth.

Verse 3 When these days commence, all kinds of dangerous creatures will emerge from their hideouts struggling to escape annihilation. In their bid for survival, they would sting and bite whoever crosses their path. In fact it is mankind they have escaped from their habitats to attack. Man is the cause of evil in Creation.

Verse 4 The seal (mark) of Dara Ndu is in His palm. Once He blesses you, the seal permeates your mind. Laying His hand on you means to disciple or teach you the true messages of the Spirit; and how best to worship It. This is indeed the seal of the Living God.

To open the seal of God therefore, is to teach mankind the sciences of Creation; show mankind how God is; and how to worship Him (the knowledge of God). Placing His (Dara Ndu's) right hand on your forehead signifies that the knowledge will be embedded in your brain (mind, intellect, memory).

First Night: Those who do not have the seal of God, which Dara Ndu brings, will be tortured. The purpose would not be to have them killed but to make them repent and worship God in Truth and Spirit. Those who do not have the seal of Dara Ndu – which is the seal of the Living God – are those who rejected the message of Spirit brought by Dara Ndu. These people will be attacked by locusts (demons) that will be unleashed upon mankind.

Verse 5-6 This is called the *Day of Apparition – the day of Reckoning.* You will see how you have wronged God. You will see your deed in apparition; how you have offended the Spirit in yourself and fellow human beings. This will happen on the first day and night of Darkness. You will pass judgment for and by yourself from the apparition, for it will appear like a *vision* and all your deeds will be glaring before you.

Verse 7-11 The locusts (demons) are angels or thoughts of God. They are demons because they are to execute activities or actions (Will of the Almighty) man does not like. These so-called demons can take any form—locusts, horses, man – God wants to use to execute His Anger. They are described here as Angel of Death.

They are called locust because they are *uncountable* (*'igwuribe'* in Igbo parlance). Locust is not the specific name of that animal species. But its name is derived from the magnitude and awesome devastation they will unleash upon mankind during this night.

Spiritually, these locusts are monstrous powers released upon man on the first day and night of destruction. These monsters will attack those people who are reluctant to chant OM Dara Ndu!!

Take a look again at the scriptural description of these locusts *(verse 7-11)*. They are battle ready; and there is no escape for mankind. The latter is doomed for destruction.

Second Night: verse 13-21 During the second night, those without the seal i.e. the message of the Messiah, will be exterminated, *Chapter 16.*

Verse 17: this is the biblical/scriptural confirmation of Dara Ndu's (physical) seal. Wherever this seal is pasted, the inhabitants are protected. No evil shall befall them—as long as they abhor evil. The Law of Attraction of

Homogeneous Species will apply here: if you do evil within the vicinity, the seal will attract more evil for you.

The *horses* symbolize Power with which the riders operate– the power with which the message is given. It is with the same power that the disciples of Jesus were sent on Evangelism. The New Testament recorded that Jesus rode on a donkey or colt (young horse). That was a revelation. Jesus never physically rode on a donkey or horse. It was not feasible at that time. Riding on a donkey signifies that Jesus moved with power.

The breastplates were for protection because they (the riders– angels of God) are judging the World. But the on-going true Message of the Spirit is already the Judgment upon mankind. There will never be a time all mankind will fall into a single file and be separated into goats and sheep according to *Matthew 25:31-34.* Those that accept the message of Dara Ndu are the sheep whereas the goats are those that reject it.

And so *Judgment has just begun. Separation has also commenced with the teachings and messages of Dara Ndu.* Dara Ndu has already ascended His Throne from where He issues out the Judgment (Messages) to the World.

When the New Testament records that Jesus was whipping the people inside the Synagogue, it refers to the sharp, but blunt and painful words of Truth He unleashed upon the people. He never physically whipped anybody. He couldn't have. That story was a revelation.

The colors: Red, Sky Blue and Yellow are the Foundation of Creation. Red represents Fire; Blue symbolizes Water; Yellow stands for Light. These are the foundation of all colors – the primary colors. This explains the color combination in the New Seal of God which Dara Ndu came with. Water and Fire are the two uncreated beings/things that formed the foundation upon which all living things were created.

And so the authority of these riders is from the Supreme Spirit. Their authority (and Power) is a True one.

CHAPTER 10 – UNVEILING THE NEW EARTH

Verse 1-3 this is the picture of the form of the Messiah and the Almighty God.

Verse 5-8 The mysterious plan refers to the New Earth that will arise after the Third Day of the Tribulation. This plan had since been announced or prophesied by the prophets.

Verse 9-10 *Scroll* (always folded and sealed) refers to the hidden message of the Spirit (God). It is the heart of the Spirit. Recall the *Tablets of the Ten Commandments*. The scroll cannot be deciphered by all-comers. It must be interpreted by the one who is in the Spirit.

Hence, when the message of the Spirit is heard, it appeals to the mind; but its application is difficult.

CHAPTER 11 – PAST REVELATION OF THE DEATH OF JOHN THE BAPTIST AND JESUS

Verse 1-13 these events have taken place in the past.

Verse 1-10: the two (2) prophets (witnesses) refer to John the Baptist and Jesus Christ of Nazareth. Jesus and John the Baptist are the two (2) renowned and recognized Prophets. Other so-called 'prophets' are mere servants of God. Their death was celebrated by mankind. Both were murdered and their bodies displayed in the public: John the Baptist was beheaded; Jesus was crucified.

All these events occurred at the end of time; hence 1,260 days or 9 (i.e. 1+2+6+0) symbolizes last days; 42 months or 6 (i.e. 4+2) talks about last events.

Verse 11-12 Jesus resurrected after 3 days; John the Baptist was translated to heaven.

This revelation had occurred and recorded in several other places and times such as New Testament, and Isaiah Chapter 53.

Verse 14-19 This is a continuation of the revelation of the end time. All created things worship the Lord.

CHAPTER 12 THE BATTLE OF THE SPIRIT, MIND AND BODY

Verse 1 This is a description of the Universal Being– the totality of the Almighty Being. The entire Universe is represented herein. *Moon and Sun* symbolize Water and Fire respectively– the two uncreated beings; and water is the foundation of all that were created. *Stars* represent all the eyes of the other creatures, with exception of Man. Whereas, Sun represent male human beings– *Anya nwa oku (anya-anwu),* Moon represents female human beings – *O, anya nwa ami (Onwa).*

Verse 2 *Purpose* of the mysterious pageant (great wonder): She has a plan– to be delivered of her pregnancy for a son. The *"Son"* symbolizes the Messiah, the Message– the birth of New Knowledge. The Supreme Spirit wants to send the Messiah down to the earth to teach and salvage mankind.

Verse 3 *The Red Dragon* represents dangerous and sophiscated creative *MIND* that will mold atomic and nuclear weapons of mass destruction. The *Seven heads* are nations or continents. The *Horns* (10 in number) refer to these nations' physical powers (of money, politics, military, education, science and technology etc.) The *Crowns* are their achievements and feats (economic and physical development).

The Continents (nations) and Share of the Powers

Nations	*Powers*
Asia	2
America	2
Europe	2
Other nations	1 each

Verse 4 (a) *Tail* refers to what these powerful nations manufactured with their money and resources. '*To cast or plunge the stars down to the earth*' means that those products would force everybody to become carnal and materialistic.

Verse 4 (b) These material things intended to swallow the 'Son' as soon as he is delivered. The Continents of America, Europe and Asia are on 'ground' everywhere: their influence permeates and pervades all nooks and crannies of the globe. When the Messiah is born, they will teach him to abandon His Purpose and embrace their materialism.

Verse 5-6 After delivery, the *Mind* snatched the boy away from the woman. But after all these *sufferings in the Mind*, the son will appear at the end time or last days, i.e. the Messiah will appear at the end of time or end of the era (1,260 days or 1+2+6+0=9). Number 9 (nine) is the last digit according to sciences of numbers–signifying end time or last days.

Verse 7-9 the battle of the Spirit, Mind and Body ensued: *Michael* and company represent the Spirit while the Dragon and host represent the Mind. This battle takes place physically, every day in everybody: *Shall I follow the Spirit or the body?*

If the Mind does not follow the Spirit, it will naturally come down to embrace the body. That is what is meant when it is said that *Lucifer* was dropped or chased down to the earth. *Lucifer* here describes the recalcitrant and disobedient Mind.

That "*war broke out in heaven*" means the Mind refuses to embrace the Spirit. If your mind cannot embrace the

Spirit, there is bound to be trouble. At this point, the latter will compel the former to follow the dictates of the body – carnality.

The Army of the Mind (*Dragon*) are the senses, the intellect, the memory, the intelligence and the body etc.

Verse 10-11 Before a man conquers his Mind, he must embrace the teachings of the Spirit from the Messiah.

Verse 12 All the negativities that manufacture the atomic bombs and other weapons of mass destruction will be at rage everywhere, to deceive people. But they have little time left. That is the reason they are raging in anger, resulting in massive production and deployment/testing of dangerous weapons.

Verse 13 the Spirit uses different forms to explain its activity namely the Supreme Spirit, the Mind and the body.

W*oman* here symbolizes the body: women always think negatively. They are possessed with fear. They are afraid of the Truth. Once you tell a woman the truth about a thing, you have created problems for yourself. If you tell her lies (provided she did not find out), she loves you the more. You will tell her a greater lie the day she finds out the truth, and her love for you increases. This is the nature of women.

Verse 14-17 The Mind created sufferings for the body. Out of rage, the Mind proceeded to attack everybody on earth, including those who have accepted the teachings of the Spirit.

Summary: this Chapter describes the battle between the Spirit and the Mind: to possess the body. The Spirit wants to use the body for *Salvation*; the Mind wants the body for *Materialism.* See *Galatians Chapter Five.*

CHAPTER 13– PROPHECIES ON BRITAIN AND UNITED STATES OF AMERICA

Verse 1.*The Beast or Strange Creature* that rose up out of the Sea refers to Earth and Mankind living therein. The Seven (7) heads refer to the seven Continents of the World. The Horns are the physical powers (money, education, science and technology etc.) possessed by these nations. The Crowns are their achievements and feats (economic and physical development) – see Chapter 12:3

The *blasphemous names* refer to insulting names of God as inscribed, for instance, on United States Dollars: *In God We Trust.* Americans worship, and trust money more than God.

Verse 2 The mind created and built all these powers (money, computers, skyscrapers, industries, automobiles etc.) on the earth.

Verse 3 *First Beast*: Britain (Europe) – The *wounded head* (nation) refers to Europe (Britain). Indeed, Europe was the first World. It had, however collapsed but later recovered. For instance Pound Sterling of Great Britain seems to be the strongest and most stable foreign currency today despite the lull in its economic development and production. This is indeed a marvel to the rest of the world economies.

Verse 4 And mankind worshipped those things that were built and created by the Mind (Dragon) unto the earth (beast): cars, skyscrapers, technology, spacecraft etc. Mankind became earthly, carnal and materialistic: "*they worshipped the beast.*"

Verse 5-6 '*We went to the moon; we clone human beings; construct houses that touch the sky*'. Mankind (beast) became proud and arrogant, making false claims. This is what America and Russia are preoccupied with in these last days: 42 months (4+2=6).

Verse 7-10 Everybody, except those who have accepted the messages of the Messiah, compulsorily worships America and Europe via what they produce; for no man can dispense with their sciences and technology.

Verse 11 *Second Beast*: United States of America

Britain colonized the United States of America; that is why the latter was seen as a lamb, but more dangerous than the former (fearsome voice like the Dragon's). Also, it has more powers (two horns) than Britain.

Verse 12 America takes after Britain socially, scientifically, economically and in every aspects of national life– having being previously colonized by the latter. Nevertheless, America has made Britain relevant in the comity of nations. The former always solicits the latter's solidarity in its war against its enemy nations.

Verse 13 the United States of America deceives the World with their *"wonders"*: missiles, armaments, spacecraft, and other weapons of mass destruction etc.

Verse 14a Both nations (Britain and USA) are always in alliance, especially when America besieges its enemy nations, employing its '*wonders*' of deception. If Britain does not render its support, America would not proceed with those escapades (Vietnam, Afghanistan, Iraq wars and domination of United Nations Assembly).

Verse 14b **Great Statue (image of the beast)** America made Britain remain relevant among world economies by rating its (Britain's) currency high among other world currencies. British Pound Sterling remains the strongest and the most sought-after foreign currency in the world. Their economic blueprints, educational system etc. are envy of other nations.

However, it was the Word of God (*Sword* – KJV) i.e. Christianity– that destabilized European powers. Anglican and Roman Catholic Churches divided the nation, resulting into unending wars. At the end of these battles, Europe was never the same again. That was the genesis of its collapse and fall as a Continent.

At this juncture, USA waded in and brokered reconciliation. They took away Christianity– accounting for the heavy concentration of clergymen and women in the United States today.

Verse 15 Any nation that does not worship Britain (now empowered and strengthened), will surely experience economic setback: Britain, in connivance with the United States of America, presides over the most powerful international organizations such as International Monetary Fund, World Bank, United Nations, WHO.

Verse 16 *"Mark"* refers to the United States Dollars and British Pound Sterling.

Verse 17 *"Name of the Beast"* refers to the individual or person whose head and name appear on the surface of the currency.

Verse 18 *"666"* is the number of the beast name (verse 17); number of the beast; and number of a man (verse 18). According to the sciences of numbers, '666' must be reduced to a single digit thus: 6+6+6=18; 1+8=9. Number '9' is the last numerical digit signifying end time, end of an era or last days – when mankind becomes mundane and carnal. See *verses 17 and 18 in Good News Bible version.*

CHAPTER 14 – PICTURE OF FINAL JUDGMENT

Verse 1 The 144,000 are the servants of the Lord who had the seal or mark of the Lord, His messages and teachings. They know the Lord. They are the nine (9) Apostles of Dara Ndu.

Verse 2-3 Of the entire mankind, only those nine Apostles are given the power to preach the Good News– the new message from Dara Ndu, the new name of the Lord (*new song*).

Verse 4 Virginity here does not imply celibacy, continence or compulsory abstinence from healthy and appropriate sex relationship with opposite sexes.

Any of these artificial/unnatural practices could tantamount to anti-creation, anti-nature, anti-God. It is only an impotent, a frigid or eunuch that can be denied sex. However, such an aberration does not make him/her a complete individual. Such a person must come back via reincarnation to fully experience life as a genuine and complete human being.

Genitals are meant for sexual intercourse just like hands, eyes and ear, etc. are given for their respective functions. Any attempt to impose an artificial or unnatural restriction on any part of the body will render such organ (s) dysfunctional and atrophied; thereby working against the Laws of the Spirit.

Sexual Continence does not guarantee spirituality. What counts is proper understanding and application of the true message of the Spirit. The Kingdom of God has nothing to do with flesh and blood. *The Living Bible (TLB) Version* correctly captures Virginity as *Spiritual Un-defilement.*

Virginity here therefore refers to Unblemished and Untouched/Untainted message of God. Those who receive this pure message are '*virgins.*'

Verse 8 '*Babylon is fallen*': Babylon refers to the human thoughts or mind; all material natures and the creations of man– sciences, technology, and the entire world system. All have collapsed. Mankind will be disappointed because the works of their hands will fail them. They became attached to materialism and forgot their source– the Spirit.

Verse 9-12 '*Mark*' here refers to money. Anybody who becomes attached to money and '*images*' (what money can buy) will suffer God's anger.

Verse 13 '*The dead which die in the Lord*' (Martyrs) refer to the 144,000 or nine Servants of Dara Ndu.

Verse 15 the '*Sickle*' refers to the Words of the Spirit. After He, the Messiah has completed the teachings (pronouncement of the Judgment), He will go into the Spirit and command His executors – angels of death – to effect the Judgment. He will accomplish this by pouring out His anger upon mankind; for He is the Angel of Death, the Storm, the Thunder and the Earthquakes etc. See *Revelation Chapter 16*.

CHAPTER 15- LINEAGE OF MESSIAHS – THE CHRIST

Verse 3 They did not sing the song of Elijah, John the Baptist, Abraham, Jeremiah nor Ezekiel. They were singing the song of *Moses* and *Jesus* – the immediate past Messiahs. Both are identical.

CHAPTER 16- THE DAY OF THE ANGER OF THE LORD

This chapter should be read in conjunction with the *Book of Amos Chapter 5:18-20*. The story describes the Second Night of the Three Days and Nights of Darkness. See *Revelation 9:13-21*

Verse 10 '*Throne (Seat) of the Beast from the Sea*' refers to the Earth.

The Holy Mother, The Blessed Virgin Mary had warned that mankind should place less attachment to materialism. They have unfortunately, but at their own doom, replaced God with matter. *See Luke 17:26-36; Matthew 24:29*

CHAPTER 17– THE EARTH, NATIONS, KINGS AND THEIR ACTIVITIES

Verse 1 '*Prostitutes, drunken woman*' etc. refers to the earth. Remember that mother or Beast can also be used to describe the earth, depending on what the Spirit wants to display. Recall the expressions: Mother Earth, Beast of the Earth, Earthly.

Verse 2 Everything the earth has produced (materialism) leads to immorality.

Verse 3-8 '*Woman sitting upon a Scarlet (red) colored beast*' describes the earth and the activities (*red*) of its mankind. The idiomatic expression: '*painting the street red*', talks about the degree of activities and events that took place.

Verse 9-13 the five (5) fallen Kings/Heads are United Kingdom, Egypt, Greek Empire, Roman Empire, and USSR. The sixth (6th) that now reigns is United States of America. The seventh (7ᵗʰ) that is yet to come is Asian Tiger (China, Japan, Korea etc.)

Verse 14 ***Fate of Dara Ndu: Prophecy on the mission of Dara Ndu***. See *Chapter 19:19-21*. Compare this with the fate of Jesus Christ of Nazareth as recorded in *Isaiah 53*.

Verse 16 the nations and their kings will hate the earth. They will no longer like to live therein. Mankind will grudge and condemn the earth. This is an attack in the Spirit– "*Let the world be destroyed.*" Very bad and dangerous thought forms!

Verse 17 God will capitalize on this terrible and evil mind/thought of mankind to bring about the destruction on earth eventually.

Verse 18 the woman represents the earth. See *chapter 13:1*

CHAPTER 18- FALL OF WORLD SUPER POWERS

Verse 1-3 This is a description of the earth, its nations and activities of mankind. See *Chapter 17*.

Verse 4-23 Collapse and Fall of USA, Europe and some part of Asia: only Africa via Nigeria will remain after the great holocaust. Nigeria is the center of action.

Verse 24 It was in USA and Europe that so many Christians were martyred.

CHAPTER 19 – EMERGENCE OF A NEW EARTH

Verse 6-9 *'Bride'* here is the New Earth peopled by the salvaged few. The *'Lamb'* is the Messiah. The *'Wedding Feast'* is the Pass over Feast (Exodus 12). It is the passing over of those that survived the Third Day of Nights of Darkness into the Golden Age (next Millennium).

Verse 10 Apostle John wanted to worship the *'projection of the Spirit,'* but it stopped him. The Spirit rather encouraged him to worship the Supreme Spirit inside him (John).

Verse 11 *'White horse'* means Righteous Power. The *'Rider'* is one who came with Righteous Power, i.e. the Messiah. *'That He justly punishes and makes war (TLB) or in righteousness he doth judge and make war (KJV)'* means that He teaches the truth; fights through His Message of Truth. In fact He disarms you with the truth, thereby putting you to shame and ridicule.

Verse 12 *'His eyes were as a flame of fire'* means He sees you with eyes of Love; eyes of Knowledge. *'Crowns'* represents His Achievements, Feats, and Conquests. They represent the flags around the Throne of Dara Ndu:

	Crowns	*Color of the flags*
1	Peace	Blue
2	Love	Red
3	Righteousness	Yellow
4	Truth	White

5	Glory (Attraction)	Purple
6	Power	Pink
7	Joy	Green

The name written on His (Dara Ndu's) forehead is the new name He bears. See *chapter 3:12*; 2:17

Verse 13 '*He was clothed with garment dipped in blood*' means He wears red clothes. And His name is called the *Word of God*. But only He knew its meaning (v.12):

The Word of God is the '*Truth*', and truth is '*Life*'. Interpreted in Igbo language, it means: *Okwu Chukwu bu Ezi Okwu; Mana Ezi Okwu bu NDU*. Jesus had previously given this revelation/hint in John 14:6, "I am the way, the *Truth and the Life*…"

What about *DARA*? According to John 1:1, "In the beginning was the *Word* and the Word was God, and the Word was with God." Here, '*Beginning*' means '*First*'. Indeed DARA is an ancient Igbo expression for '*First*'.

On the other hand, the Word is OM! OM is the combination of O + M, derived from the two Igbo expressions '*Oku na Mmiri (Fire and Water)* – the First Two Uncreated Beings that constituted the foundation of Creation (Genesis 1:2); the entities the Universe worship as The Spirit. Therefore OM is First or Dara; as well as the Spirit.

Paraphrasing John 1:1, "In the beginning was OM and the OM was the Spirit and OM was the First Word of The Spirit.

In a nutshell, Dara Ndu means '*First that is Life*'. But the First Being that is Life is the Supreme Spirit. Therefore, DARA NDU is the WORD of GOD – the new name of Christ, the Messiah.

Verse 15 The *sharp sword* represents the Truth…that will disorganize the deceptive and misleading world system. For instance, Man did not and cannot go to the Moon, etc.

That He will '*rule with iron rod*' means He will rule with strictness (not wickedness): insisting on strict obedience to the Laws of the Spirit. Remember the rod of iron does not bend. It is straight. The Messiah will rule with Righteousness and Justice.

'*He trod the winepress of the fierceness…*' signifies that all that were hidden will be revealed by the anger of God; the past deeds of every man will be exposed during those three days of nights and darkness.

Verse 17-18 The roasted carcasses of evil people will be exposed in the open.

Verse 19 Mankind, including pastors, priests and false prophets will come to challenge Dara Ndu when His Mission commences in earnest. But He will defeat them.

Verse 20 '*The Beast was captured (taken prisoner…)*': the Message of Dara Ndu disarms all persons that dare challenge Him. His messages have the potentiality to lull all confrontations and arguments to slumber. This is the Sulphur– power of the Truth/Message.

As soon as one hears Him speak, the Spirit inside him will definitely acknowledge the truth therein and immediately disarm the evil mind. That person would no longer proceed with his premeditated attack on Dara Ndu.

'*The Beast and False Prophet were thrown into the Lake of Fire that burns with Sulphur*': when these evil people acknowledge the truth at last, they will become furious and angry with themselves. They will suddenly realize they have unfortunately wasted time, money and strength building falsehood which they call churches.

Lake of Fire with Sulphur is idiomatic. Recall that Jesus whipped the Jews in the Synagogue, *Matthew 21:12*– He told them painful truth. Lake of Fire represents the Truth/Knowledge; whereas Sulphur is the power inherent in the Truth.

Verse 21 With the exuding of the Sulphur, the entire evil mankind will be '*killed*' in the Spirit. Physically, they will become tired of life and no longer pose as threats to Dara Ndu.

CHAPTER 20– CYCLE OF HUMAN ERA AND FINAL JUDGMENT

Human Era is divided into four (4) phases of 500 years each culminating into a total period of 2,000 years.

Verse 1-10 Christ, the Messiah will rule for 1,000 years while the Mind (Materialism and Carnality) will dominate for the next 1,000 years thus:

Scriptural Reference	Verses 1 to 6		Verses 7 to 9	
Authority	Christ, the Messiah		Mind/ Satan	
Name of Age	Golden	Silver	Bronze	Iron
Number of Years	500	500	500	500

That the Messiah will rule for 1,000 years means His teachings of righteousness are upheld and practiced by mankind during this time period. He may not be in the flesh for these 1,000 years, but His True Messages of righteousness will hold sway because He is the Spirit.

At the expiry of this first 1,000 years, evil will begin to infiltrate mankind. This Evil, also known as Mind or Satan will dominate mankind for another 1,000 years.

Characteristics of the Ages:

Phase	*Age*	*Percentage (%) of Righteousness*	*Percentage (%) of Evil*
First	Golden	Above 75	Below 25
Second	Silver	50	50
Third	Bronze	25	75
Fourth	Iron/Khali	Less than 5	More than 95

This cycle is repeated every 2,000 years (v.10), usually concluded with the iron age – when Christ, the messiah repeats His Advent. At Iron Age, there is always concomitant preponderance of evil and high sex perversion. Second death will be suffered by those who are influenced by this world of evil. But the Salvaged few will always reign with the Messiah for 1,000 years, (v.5).

One is therefore admonished not to receive the mark of the beast, nor worship his image and statute. One should detach himself completely from worldliness: materialism and carnality.

Verse 11-15 *At Final Judgment*, all the unsaved minds are destroyed by fire; and the salvaged few are passed over to the next millennium (Golden and Silver ages of 1,000 years).

CHAPTER 21- THE NEW EARTH

Verse 1-2 New Earth! New Heaven!! New thoughts!!! The orientation and thoughts of mankind will be *Truth, Love, Righteousness, Peace and Joy:* the true virtues of Mankind.

Nobody is living to build mansions or skyscrapers, nor acquire fleeting properties etc. Everybody lives for one another. Mankind will live communal life– life of support for one another.

The old heaven and old earth will vanish. Everything becomes new.

Verse 3-8 The Kingdom of God is within the Earth. The Kingdom of Heaven is physically on earth, but spiritually in the hearts of all living things.

Verse 9 The *Bride* is the new earth.

Verse 10-27 The *City* refers to the Kingdom of God on earth. The twelve (12) gates are the windows of the earth. The *foundation stones inlaid with gems* are the precious stones found in Israel, used to describe the beauty of the new earth (v.18).

Revelations given by the Spirit have local contents. Dara Ndu receives messages that are linked with His earthly ancestral home, Azia. If Jesus had incarnated in Ngwo, in Enugu State, Nigeria, for instance, *Okpa* (that local delicacy) would have passed for bread.

Every Messiah therefore has a local content: His name, body, location, language, culture, tradition must reflect the geographical place He incarnated.

CHAPTER 22– SALVATION (ETERNAL LIFE)

Verse 1-2 *The River of Pure Water of Life and Trees of Life* refer to the Supreme Spirit, the Messiah and His Message. The *Twelve (12) crops of fruits and leaves* represent the extent of the spread of the message. As it expands and flows from the Spirit through the mind to the body, it heals nations.

In this context therefore, the Water of Life is Spirit, God is Mind and the lamb is the body.

Verse 3-5 *City* represents the Kingdom of the Spirit and the Knowledge (message) of the Messiah. However, the city or kingdom can be translated physically as earth because the Messiah will teach physically here on earth, but spiritually in the hearts of all living things.

Verse 13 **Without Dara Ndu, there is no Salvation. Outside the message of Dara Ndu, no one earns Salvation. If you attain Dara Ndu, all achievements come to an end. He is everything – the A and Z, the beginning and the End; the First and the Last.**

Verse 14 " *washing their robes":* Salvation is a continuous process. It is not something one begins to think about on the Judgment Day.

ABOUT THE BOOK

One of the greatest challenges Jesus faced in the course of His Ministry on Earth, was the unfortunate misinterpretations of the Laws of Moses by Jewish religious leaders.

The Synoptic Gospels contain a litany of altercations between Jesus and the Jews in this direction. The Jewish religious leaders had replaced the "doctrines" of God with the "commandments of men". And through the years, these false interpretations of men had gradually taken the rightful place of the true Laws of God. In fact these incidences eventually carried a high price: they cost John the Baptist his head; and they got Jesus nailed to the cross.

Sadly today, we find that Christians are also repeating the same mistakes of the past. Bible scholars all over the World have differed in understanding of very critical Scriptural teachings– everyone dissecting the "Word" as he feels. Consequently, the Scripture suffers carnal, physical and literal interpretations in the hands of these "religious merchants". The outcome has been:

confusion, delusion, needless controversy and ignorance in the body of Christ.

In this book, Dara Ndu aims at correctly interpreting what He spoke in the Books of the Law; the Synoptic Gospels and the Revelations to Apostle John (the Beloved).

Understanding the Real Teachings of Moses and Jesus is a reference book; and therefore it is recommended to be read alongside the Bible. And as you study the Bible with this book, you will be "translated" out of the "darkness" of ignorance and misinterpretations of the Word of God into the light of the true "Faith".

ABOUT THE AUTHOR

Emeka Ude, J. was born in the Eastern part of Nigeria. He studied Accountancy and Finance in Nigerian Universities; and currently enrolled for Ph. D (Accounting) in one of the prestigious Universities overseas. He is an Associate member of Institute of Chartered Accountants of Nigeria. He is a Banker, a Publishing and Management Consultant, an Author and Teacher.

His love for deep spiritual knowledge, which has led him to examining several great books, can easily pass him as a philosopher and mystic. His contact with the TRUTH has become the fulfillment of his call to LIFE.

Emeka Ude J. is happily married and blessed with an amazing family.

Milton Keynes UK
Ingram Content Group UK Ltd.
UKHW040837160724
445389UK00001B/23

9 781964 393513